A STONE
IN THE SHADE

VP drawing in the Red Fort, Delhi, October 1969

A STONE
IN THE SHADE

VIOLET POWELL

STONE TROUGH
BOOKS

ISBN 978 0 9544542 8 9

Published by Stone Trough Books
The Old Rectory, Settrington
York YO17 8NP

Printed and bound by
Smith Settle, Yeadon, West Yorkshire LS19 7XY

CONTENTS

ILLUSTRATIONS

FOREWORD

'I DO SEE'—these were favourite words of Violet Powell on being treated to a rambling history of social derring-do or unexpected discomfiture. To me, they were welcome words because they were sincere: Violet was really the most sympathetic audience you could have, just as she was the most sympathetic friend, quite apart from our family connection (she was my father's sister). Now these words come back to me on reading Violet's journals: she really did see, in the truest sense, and had the capacity to translate her observations into alert, interested, humorous prose, quite apart from recording it all in sketches and watercolours.

The result is a marvellously perceptive account, mainly of her travels together with the writer she married in 1934, Anthony Powell, but including various London vignettes of the time which will delight, I would have thought, future literary biographers. The focus of *A Stone in the Shade* is the cultural cruise in the shape of a Swan's Hellenic Tour. 'With singular neatness,' writes Violet, the death of Powell's father offered them 'the opportunity to change the pattern of our holiday life' : the Swan's brochure was in fact delivered by the postman just as they were dealing with the business which is the inevitable aftermath of death. Violet had long had the idea of such a cruise at the back of her mind—on her first visit to Venice as a girl, she had envied the passengers in a bobbing fleet of gondolas on their way to a cruise ship. Now she could gratify this desire. 'This made the next twenty years a time of widening horizons and intellectual enjoyment,' in Violet's words, starting with the first cruise on the *SS Ankara*, aptly named 'The Pearl of the Mediterranean' which took in Sardinia, North Africa and Malta before reaching Greece.

I myself had the good luck to join the Powells on one cruise, led by Sir Mortimer Wheeler, in the spring of 1961. The relish and enjoyment displayed by both Tony and Violet at shipboard life, as well as the ancient sights we were there to admire, stays with me still. As does my own embarrassment, rooted like so many similar episodes in my failure to admit ignorance at the beginning. Tony suggested that in order to discuss our shipboard companions in an amusingly coded fashion, we should dub them with the names of characters from Scott Fitzgerald; at some point *The Great Gatsby* was mentioned specifically. I don't think I went so far as to declare that I had read it (I hadn't) while Tony simply assumed my knowledge. In any case I was doing just fine bluffing my way through, until I answered some stray remark about a certain Jordan with a spirited disquisition on the character, based on the erroneous assumption that Jordan Baker was a man... It was Violet who gently disillusioned me in the most tactful way with a carefully phrased remark which made my mistake obvious to me while not specifically correcting it. And it was greatly to Tony's credit that he made no comment at the time, simply switched his comparisons to characters from Dickens, where he rightly supposed that even I could not make a fool of myself.

On the one hand, these diaries are full of the kind of detail which evokes the period; on the other hand there are adventures enough to satisfy, one would suppose, Lady Hester Stanhope, although without the need to take up residence in the area afterwards. The fact that Swan cruises invariably carried an Anglican chaplain illustrates the former point. Yet although the book and its delightful illustrations are focussed on travel, there are plenty of other vignettes of the Powells' English life, and Violet's Anglo-Irish childhood. The reader is amused to discover that Anthony Powell was 'allergic to manifestations of (his wife's) Irish background,' but fortunately Violet has too much spirit to pay much attention to that. Here for example, are the beggars who alarmed her mother, coming from sedate Oxfordshire, by crowding round the front door of what was known locally as the Castle (actually Pakenham Hall) in Westmeath. Mary Julia, widowed Countess of Longford, attempted to persuade the locals that begging should be done strictly at the side doors, of which there was an inordinate number. 'The result was that a black-shawled figure might be found at any doorstep' including that of the front door. Given the imposing nature of Pakenham Hall (rechristened Tullynally by the present owner), this anecdote seems to me to sum up the dual nature of the Anglo-Irish aristocracy—loftily removed and close to the peasantry at one and the same time.

In this connection, Violet tells one story in which the peasantry became unexpectedly relevant. It begins with a vivid sketch of Dorothy Sayers, a substantial figure with a *pince nez* wearing a sleeveless gown of peach velvet, which would have been a tight fit for the slimmest of girls. The famous novelist then proceeded to skid on a rug across the room while trying to inspect some of the host's treasures, to the audible gasps of the company. Further gasps were occasioned at the next dinner party where Lady Violet Powell, as an earl's daughter, was seated on the host's right, correctly taking precedence over a mere baron's wife in the shape of the flamboyant literary star Christabel Lady Aberconway. The latter was thoroughly confused by her apparent demotion, and kept addressing Violet as 'Mrs. Powell' throughout the meal, to express her dissatisfaction. The host's sister Edith Sitwell tried to right the situation by explaining who Violet was, and more to the point, who her family were. The result was an enquiry to 'Mrs. Powell' from Christabel Aberconway, by no means enlightened: 'And do you have some wonderful Irish peasant blood?'

There are of course many stories and asides which will satisfy the devotees of *A Dance to the Music of Time*, like myself—the fact that discreet references might be made in the Powell household to 'a Widmerpool' for example. At the same time, this is a book to be savoured above all for the character of the writer herself. 'I do see.' Yes, Violet Powell saw a great deal and was able to capture it with a pen that both wrote and sketched with her own special mixture of sympathy, humour and vitality.

ANTONIA FRASER

SS Ankara at Syracuse, 1960

INTRODUCTION TO
THE *SS ANKARA*

IT IS UNUSUAL for deaths not to leave an emotional hangover, and the death of my father-in-law Philip Powell, Lt-Colonel, the Welch Regiment, was no exception. He was approaching his seventy-eighth birthday and in the six years since his wife's death had been essentially rudderless. He had died on New Year's Eve 1959 which created a number of awkwardnesses for the hotel on Richmond Hill where he had ended his days. Even the soberest of hotels feels it necessary to offer some form of celebration to guests who may wish to see in the New Year. Consequently the undertakers had to be held back until the last revellers had gone to bed.

Although he had latterly been on rocky terms with the manageress, he had not been entirely without his partisans, mostly ladies with whom he was on rather flirtatious terms. His last known act was to give a copy of *Lolita* to one of these fellow hotel-dwellers. It was our great good luck that he never, as far as we knew, proposed marriage to any of them. As a sop to the manageress we gave her my father-in-law's radio gramophone. She must have been pleased to see the last of the Powell family.

Among other relics we removed was my mother-in-law's work basket. It seemed that she never came home without having bought a reel of coloured cotton. To this day I reap the benefit of this habit, and even more so that among the cotton reels a pretty diamond clasp had become entangled. Colonel Powell had also preserved a collection of photographs from the days when he had belonged to a camera club which supplied models including girls in various states of undress.

The interview with Colonel Powell's bank manager, on whom it was not unknown for him to call more than once a day, was unexpectedly satisfactory. The manager's good-bye—'Now you will be worrying about surtax'—was probably a valediction to a customer who had the eccentric idea of being kind to his bank by keeping an inordinately large balance in his current account.

The funeral, on 4th January 1960, was limited to immediate family and Colonel Powell's sister Katherine Bonsey who had cherished a dependent relationship with her younger brother. Extremely good-looking, even in advanced years, her life had been a slow-moving disaster. As a girl she had been courted by a young man who had arrived at Melton Mowbray with two or three hunters, which indicated that he had the means to support a wife.

The atmosphere at The Elms, Melton Mowbray, had elements of Robert S. Surtees, crossed with Ivy Compton-Burnett.

Lionel Lewis Powell, Anthony's grandfather, was a surgeon, much addicted to hunting. He was the character from Surtees and living at Melton provided him with both pleasure and a supply of patients injured on the hunting field. Jessie, his wife, could have passed into a Compton-Burnett novel with no adjustment as a self-indulgent fantasist. Their daughter Katherine, 'Kitten', was distinctly neglected but both parents encouraged the attentions of young Arthur Bonsey until it was revealed that both his hunters belonged to an uncle to whom he acted as agent.

The Powells immediately backtracked. Kitten must not encourage a penniless suitor already enlisted to go to the South African War. Suppose he returned with a wooden leg? No girl of spirit would have resisted such a challenge. When Bonsey returned intact Kitten eloped, only to find that her parents had been right in the long run. She found herself abandoned, with three sons to bring up. Consequently she came to rely on her brother for male support, so that his death left her bereft. The Welch Regiment sent a wreath to the funeral, and appropriately at the moment of the burial a local quarry fired an unusually loud explosion, a salute to someone who had been a soldier for most of his grown-up life.

As Tristram remarked, it had been a very emotional vacation, but with singular neatness we were offered an opportunity to change the pattern of our holiday life. This made the next twenty years a time of widening horizons and intellectual enjoyment. It was while we were straightening out the aftermath of business contingent on a death that the postmen delivered the brochure of Swan's Hellenic Tours. These cruises had been, as it were, in the back of my mind since my first visit to Venice in 1929. Then, from the security of the Hotel Europa, I had watched a fleet of bobbing gondolas taking passengers to the *Stella d'Italia.*

Now it seemed possible that this was a holiday on which we could take John as he did not object to sleeping in a dormitory, having done so at his prep school. The bill of fare for this cruise was not limited to the isles of Greece and its mainland. The *SS Ankara*, 'Pearl of the Mediterranean', sailed from Genoa and took in Sardinia, North Africa and Malta, before reaching Greek waters.

The prospect seemed all the more enjoyable when snow fell, which in the Mendips can disrupt the best laid plans. Heavy snow, in my experience, leads to two days of panic hibernation, after which inconvenience casts out fear. This particular winter's fall was not so serious as I had expected. At that date we had town and country tyres fixed to our motor-car. These allowed us to sail up Railford, the final hill on the way home to Chantry, passing post-vans and other assorted vehicles. Shortly afterwards, these town and country tyres were banned for reasons of safety most inconsiderate to what in Ireland would be called 'mountainy' men.

The snow was not persistent and I seemed to have had a marathon socially in London just after St Valentine's Day. At this time I was particularly fortunate in having the run of my sister Mary Clive's apartment. This included the two top floors of a house in Cadogan Gardens, Chelsea, taken as a starting-point for—to quote Henry James—'the first social steps of that handsome and natural Alice'. (The Alice to whom James referred was actually a cousin from an earlier generation, but the quotation is apposite.)

Next door to the house of which my sister inhabited the upper stories, there was some sort of military office. From the street it was possible to see the interior's dreary décor, typical of such establishments and, when the lights were on, to read the almost poetical, 'Let security be your watchword.' Upstairs from next door, burglars did once force an entry into the Clives' flat but retired empty-handed, George Clive's interesting purchases of modern art not being to their taste.

As the 1960s moved into the 1970s I became aware that, at that magical hour when an evening's engagements move from drinks to dinner, an old friend could be seen outside the block of flats, obviously looking for a taxi. This old friend, Cyril Connolly, mysterious and curiously romantic, always seemed to be slightly fussed on these occasions. Preoccupied with my own plans for the evening, I only wondered vaguely on whom Cyril might be calling, only later to learn that I had been watching a passage in Connolly's last attachment. This was all in the future. In early 1960 Cyril had only just belatedly become the owner of what he considered to be a chief Enemy of Promise, 'the pram in the hall'.

Another pleasure of the flat in Cadogan Gardens came from listening to the early morning clatter of hooves as the Household Cavalry rode out, exercising from the not-too-distant Knightsbridge Barracks. The troopers rode bareback through the empty streets when the only touch of colour came from their cap bands. My father's great-uncle, General Sir Edward Pakenham, had served with distinction under his brother-in-law the 1st Duke of Wellington in the Peninsular. Less happily he commanded, and died, at the disastrous siege of New Orleans. He was, however, commemorated in a public house, The Pakenham, reached by an alleyway opposite Knightsbridge Barracks. Lifeguards are notoriously magnets to some members of their own sex. It was, in my still unmarried days, interesting to learn that 'hanging about round the Pakenham' did not imply admiration for any female of my family. My great-uncle Ned had also attached to his memory the far from rare legend that his body had been shipped home in a cask of spirits which, on reaching the home port, was found to have been drained and drunk by the ship's company.

As Anthony wished to place a memorial to his parents in Chantry Church, they being buried in the churchyard, he invited David

Kindersley, famous designer of alphabets, to stay for a night and discuss the question. At the moment Mr Kindersley was due to arrive I inquired, 'What will he look like?' Anthony replied, 'He will have a long red beard.' There was immediately a knock on the door but the first moments of the artist's visit were slightly strained by my efforts to repress my giggles. In 1960 beards were something of a rarity but the one cultivated by David Kindersley was a particularly fine example of the long and red.

To obtain from the Diocese a faculty to install a memorial can be compared to shaking a tree of unripe fruit, but the Kindersley design on slate was at length accepted. Among its admirers was the widow of our late rector who had once accused me of causing her husband to break out in psychosomatic shingles when I blocked his attempt to burn the rood screen of Chantry Church. I was pleased when she asked from whom the memorial had been commissioned, and accepted the enquiry as an olive branch.

The Swan Hellenic Cruise (No. 18, 2nd to 18th April 1960), the first on which we sailed, was also a new enterprise in that it included calls at the North African ports of Tunis and Tripoli. As so often before a holiday I felt that collapse was only an hour away, but meeting the party at Heathrow to fly to Milan revived my spirits with its congenial promise. Sir Mortimer Wheeler was to be the leading tour lecturer; Sir Maurice Bowra the leading classical academic.

Mortimer Wheeler (his friends called him Rik, an abbreviation of Eric) had once previously crossed my path, an unusually accurate description of our meeting. Shortly before the Second World War, with a recklessness which he himself had admitted, he had married Mavis de Vere Cole, a bouncing blonde, whose affair with Augustus John was famous far beyond John's immediate circle.

Anthony had known John for years but I had only met him casually. It was at a party of Beatrice Dawson's, 'Bumble' to her familiars, and famous as a stage designer, that I happened to be discussing John's wish to paint my sister Julia (wife of Robin Mount). She was actually unkeen, apprehensive of the pass that might be expected from the painter. On my side I was deploring his tendency to encourage Julia's plumpness.

Augustus had just growled 'Never too fat for me' when the newly-married Wheelers arrived in the room. Mavis was no lightweight and her height was increased by a black top hat. Diving through the crowd and sweeping me to one side, she hurled herself upon Augustus with the enthusiasm of a labrador puppy. Wheeler stood rather helplessly in the background, giving me a look of embarrassment verging on the pathetic. I recollect his hair and moustache as being dark, but twenty years later they had lightened to grey, Mavis had disappeared from his life and he had become famous for appearances on TV, a medium ideally suited to his temperament. Our subsequent travels with Rik Wheeler on cruises developed into a friendship cemented by two month-long tours of the Indian subcontinent.

Anthony describes in his memoirs how, on this first Hellenic cruise, his rapprochement with Bowra was sealed on the long coach ride from Milan to Genoa. At first the road ran across the Lombardy plain: willow, willow all the way, and magnolias at the corners. Meanwhile John read *1066 and All That* aloud to Catherine Tennant, both of them laughing heartily.

Although, for a while, primroses and cherry blossom were added to the floral display, the last hour was made hellish by a series of tunnels through the Ligurian Alps. An additional horror was the upsurge of the production from the Fiat works, towering above us on double-decker transporters.

One of the more esoteric pleasures of a Swan Cruise ceased when all passengers were taken by air to the port of departure. No longer did those on board have the interest of a special train draw up alongside the *SS Ankara*. In 1960, however, Anthony, John and I watched the advance of a number of friends over the railway lines on the quay at Genoa. Andrew and Debo Devonshire had brought their children Peregrine and Emma, Edward and Kitty Mersey had brought their son Andrew, a party that provided high drama before the cruise was over.

John slept in a male dormitory where each passenger had two births, the spare one acting as a depository for clothes. Anthony and I had an inside cabin which I compared to sleeping on a moped but it was otherwise not inconvenient. The *Ankara* being a Turkish ship, two of the crew added an exotic touch by spreading their prayer mats and kneeling bowed towards Mecca outside our cabin door.

After a couple of cruises I studied the plan of the cabins and discovered that the lowest deck had an unusually large proportion of lavatories allocated to females. In future we booked accordingly. This increased comfort because the majority of women passengers were singularly inept at managing the plumbing. I could only admire the great R. K. Swan's handling of a complaint on this question of failing to pull plugs: 'My dear Madam, I entirely agree with you, but there is absolutely nothing I can do about it.'

Our first call was in Sardinia. Prowling round Cagliari, John happened on a plaque commemorating the visit of D. H. Lawrence who was in the habit of losing each new Paradise soon after he had reached it. I believe that Sardinia was one that he lost almost immediately on arrival. I noted that lemons in Sardinia were twice life size, but that does not seem to have attracted Lawrence.

Crossing to Tunis we spent the morning in Carthage, Maurice Bowra, Anthony and I deciding that the time had come to revive the cult of Tanit. This was far from the view of Catherine Tennant. With a frisson of horror she explained that one of the lecturers had told that Tanit (a distinctly snobbish goddess) only accepted the sacrifice of well-born children but was prepared to be placated by those up to Catherine's age of twelve.

The North African coast had not then been tidied up nor trampled on by the feet of many tourists. This was particularly true of Leptis Magna, where some of us paddled among the golden stones, and golden orioles flitted through the bushes.

On the whole, Swan cruisers tended to be divided between British and American in equal numbers, but in 1960 there was also an erudite Italian, Count Grazadei. He had been a friend of Giuseppe di Lampedusa, the Sicilian nobleman who had recently died at 67, just after publishing *Il Gattopardo* (The Leopard), his first literary effort. The novel had a great success in several languages, and as a film in 1962. Count Grazadei said that Lampedusa had been inspired

7

to write a masterpiece by annoyance at some despised kinsman winning a literary prize. It was even rumoured that Lampedusa had been unwilling to change the pattern of his life on becoming a writer. Consequently he composed *Il Gattopardo* in the back room of the Syracuse café which he habitually frequented.

At an early port of call the Merseys had bought a copy of *The Times* in which it was announced that Andrew Devonshire's grandmother, the formidable Evelyn, Duchess of Devonshire, had died. She was famous for having organised the restoration of Hardwick Hall, 'more glass than wall'. As she was also famous in her family for being able to detect dry rot in an apparently sound house, she brought a useful skill to the enterprise.

Naturally Andrew had to fly home to attend his grandmother's affairs. Hardly had he returned when, at another port, the Merseys again bought a copy of *The Times* in which it was announced that Christopher Holland-Martin, husband of Andrew's aunt Anne and godfather of our son John, had died. Somewhat frivolously I suggested that it would be as well if the Merseys ceased to buy *The Times*.

These bits of sad family news were far less dramatic than the adventure which overtook some of the Devonshire family on the heights of Mount Parnassus. Emma Cavendish is a botanist of the sort that keeps Bentham and Hooker on her dressing-table, or wherever the light happens to fall, her father being an equally dedicated gardener. With a permit from the Natural History Museum to import plants with roots attached, and a supply of plastic bags, they prepared to assault Mount Parnassus where, among other rarities, the wild golden tulip is uniquely to be found.

A picnic had been organised by Mark Ogilvie-Grant and Dorothy Lygon, friends resident in Athens, but earlier members of the party dropped off and descended the mountain, reporting that the botanists were still filling their bags.

Meanwhile Anthony and I were retracing our steps along the Sacred Way which we had trodden on our honeymoon twenty-six years before. Then there had been one inn, simple but adequate, in the village of Delphi. The visitors' book had been sparsely filled, though the names of Jean and Cyril Connolly, together with that of Brian Howard and his German boyfriend, struck a familiar note. Eagles had soared in the sky above the Sacred Way, and the wonderful view to the plain, where the olive groves of Itea march beside the Adriatic, was not blocked by any building.

In 1960 the eagles still soared but an outcrop of new hotels now interfered with the view below the town. The Sacred Way and the Castalian spring had however retained the mystery which we had found when entirely alone on the site. Our only companion had been Baedeker, published in 1909 but still invaluable.

It was a long day but as the three of us were thankfully starting dinner Debo came along the deck to our table, remarking that Andrew and Emma were still on the mountain. Being near sailing time, when we saw the lights of a car on the quay, we assume that the laggard botanists had just made it. The *Ankara* sailed as scheduled, but after dinner it became known that Andrew, his daughter Emma and Edward Mersey had been left behind on Mt Parnassus with their friends from Athens. Debo, with Peregrine and another boy, had been bundled ashore at the last moment, taking toothbrushes and sweaters as emergency luggage.

Unfortunately the sealed communist state of Albania prevented any hope of the party rejoining the ship overland. But when the *Ankara* docked at Corfu the following morning, the good news came that the strayaways had been rescued by the local police, equipped to deal with Mt Parnassus in the dark. The botanists had been in the tantalising position of being able to see the *Ankara* lying off Itea but unable to find a path downwards. At one moment Edward Mersey had jumped down what he thought was the beginning of a path, only to find that he could move neither up nor down. Dorothy ('Coote') Lygon had a stout leather belt round her waist and the team together hauled him up. Night was coming on, so it was planned to huddle at their picnic spot, but there was incredulous relief when the lights of a search party illuminated the scene. It only remained to rescue the luggage and return home at considerable extra expense.

The golden tulips from Mt Parnassus survived to flower in the gardens at Chatsworth, a golden relic in more senses than one as I was unkind enough to remark.

Two days after the cruise had ended, an account of the incident appeared in two separate newspaper gossip columns. A mishap to a ducal party was obviously good copy though the incident was inconveniently free from any hint of sexual scandal. It was necessary to enliven the story by telling how the sturdy Turkish captain of the *Ankara*, unimpressed by aristocratic pressure, refused to hold up its sailing. Journalistically this was an opportunity for toff-bashing too good to be hampered by veracity.

Daily Express April 20th

William Hickey

Night on a bare mountain —by the Duke of Devonshire

WHO GOT LOST WHILE PICKING FLOWERS

ALL the Duke of Devonshire wanted to do was pick a few wild flowers. And look what happened . . . he missed his boat . . . worried his wife, . . . and spent the night under the stars in a rocky ravine. It all began when the cruise ship Ankara, in which he and his family have just made a cruise of

The duke, with his 16-year-old daughter, Lady **Emma Cavendish** and **Viscount Mersey**, joined a party climbing Mount Parnassus, led by a local guide.

Panic

On the way up the rocky path the Duke, who is a keen amateur botanist, stopped to admire some specimens that particularly fascinated him. So did Lord Mersey—and a fellow-passenger, a Mr. Brecklehurst.

By the time they had completed their researches, the party had vanished. They scrambled about, trying to find their way back to Itea and their hotel. But as darkness fell, they realised they were utterly lost in the depths of a ravine.

Meanwhile, down at Itea, the climbers had returned—without the duke and his friends. All was panic and larm.

The ship sails

The duchess and Lady Mersey insisted that search parties go out. The Ankara was due away. Its siren was sounding.

The captain was shrugging his shoulders and saying that duke or no duke he had a schedule to maintain. Not even mention of the deputy-speaker's name would stay him.

Eventually he sailed, hours late, leaving the duchess, her 15-year-old son, Lord Hartington, and Lady Mersey on the quayside.

Searchers eventually located the duke in the ravine. Cold, no doubt, and annoyed I am sure, at missing his boat, and rowing. I suspect, that in future he will

THE DUCHESS *Alarmed* . . .

not loiter too long over h flowers.

His group continued the journey to Athens by road—al from there, flew home.

"The whole thing was a mo alarming experience for them said Lord Mersey's mother, th Dowager Lady Mersey, in Londo yesterday.

"It is a very wild country ar to spend a night out there wi a most frightening business."

quite untrue

The cruise had other, more lasting, influence on the lives of some passengers. Elizabeth Glenconner took such a strong fancy to Corfu that, only seven years later, I found myself staying in the house which she and Christopher built in the next bay to Paleokastriza. Elizabeth has made a good case for this being the bay at which Ulysses came ashore, coyly shielding himself with a leafy branch when he met Nausicaä and her bathing attendants.

It was Good Friday when the *Ankara* docked at Corfu, and a lamb, to be the family's Easter dinner, was tethered outside every house in the town. Georgina Battiscombe, author of a biography of Charlotte M. Yonge, and I, a fellow devotee of the novelist, had an enjoyable discussion about Philip Morville (*The Heir of Redcliffe*) who recovered from a near-fatal attack of fever in Corfu. At that date, c.1860, the island was a British possession in which cricket and ginger beer remain to this day. There also survived a small group of Anglicans who were invited to lunch on board the *Ankara*, Swan cruises invariably carrying a Church of England chaplain.

As a result of this Swan cruise and friendship with Georgina Battiscombe I was invited to be a founder member of the Charlotte M. Yonge Society, a group which was a source of pure happiness for more than thirty-five years. After an initial meeting chaired by Marghanita Laski at her home on Windmill Hill, a fascinating house in which no two rooms were on the same level, Mrs Battiscombe entertained the society at the Guards Club. I was invited to give a paper and chose 'Miss Yonge's Taste in Dress' as a subject. Among the examples I gave was that of Lady Rosamund Charnock (*The Three Bridges*) who is described as coming down to dinner in what I called 'rather grubby separates'. There was hearty—perhaps too hearty—laughter when I added that I had always been made uneasy by Miss Yonge's low opinion of the standard of grooming prevalent among daughters of Irish earls.

2.

CLOSING ACCOUNTS

THE LOSS of Constant Lambert, a friend from his early days in London, was one that Anthony felt irreparable, and so it turned out to be. Their friendship was of the sympathetic kind summed up by Montaigne when talking of Etienne de la Boëtie, 'Parce que c'était lui, parce que c'était moi.' Since Constant's death in 1951, there had been various suggestions of a biography. The difficulty seemed to be that a writer who could grasp the essence of Constant's personality, respect the somewhat convoluted feelings of the surviving family, and give weight to the musical genius of the subject, was hard to find. To give an example, a possible biographer, with musical qualifications, was felt to be ill-suited to the task when he was known to have expressed bewilderment about disharmony in marriage. He had been married for more than ten years and it had been a honeymoon all the way

This reversion to the loss of Constant occurs because 1960 was the year in which *Casanova's Chinese Restaurant* was published. Anthony had reflected before deciding that, as no biography of Lambert had yet been commissioned, the appearance of Hugh Moreland in *Casanova's Chinese Restaurant* could not only be accepted as a memorial to friendship but also as a tribute to genius.

During the spring of 1960 it became clear that there was likely to be a further closing of accounts besides the death of Colonel Powell. Creative artists are spared the pains of compulsory retirement at an age dictated by a profession, but they do not always escape the cruel moment when their life as an artist ebbs away and they are left on a barren shore. This tragic deprivation overtook Henry Lamb, husband of my sister Pansy, who died in the October of that year.

Anthony and I drove over to his funeral at the village church of Coombe Bissett. On the way we met two coaches bearing the proud label, Bournemouth Philharmonic Orchestra. Lamb, it could be said, had cared as deeply for music as he had for painting, perhaps even more, as music did not require him to trim his sails to professional commitments. He had frequented concerts and opera in Bournemouth, and after a performance of *Figaro* he had enlivened my posing for him by singing, 'All I said, Sir, of Cherubino, was pure conjecture.' To meet the BPO was a moving part of a farewell to Henry.

The funeral itself had echoes of the long ago in the presence of Augustus and Dorelia John. In the early 1900s Augustus had removed Lamb's first wife, Euphemia, while Lamb had loved Dorelia with a deep and lasting devotion. Dorelia, always beautiful and enigmatic, did perhaps look sad. Augustus, on the other hand, looked far from mournful. He even remarked that the funeral had been an enjoyable occasion.

In the same month Anne Holland-Martin, whose husband Christopher had died while we were on the Hellenic cruise in the spring, had asked us to visit her at Colwall. This pretty red-brick house had been bought by Anne and Christopher when he was elected MP for Ludlow. Anne was now living there, forlornly, as a widow. Anthony found it would be possible to combine this visit with digging among his Welsh roots on the hills above Hay-on-Wye.

Anne's other guest was Godfrey Winn, an immensely successful columnist in a women's weekly. When Anthony had worked in the publishers Duckworths he had the job of editing Godfrey Winn's novels. Winn himself had been a schoolboy tennis champion, but also a figure in disreputable stories in which male brothels were apt to occur. On the other hand his novels were strictly heterosexual, deviations treated with shocked disapproval.

As it happened, I had eaten some oysters a few days before, and I think for that reason I was obliged to flee from dinner, remaining supine for the next twenty-four hours. Recovery set in, but the allergy to oysters did, alas, persist. Meanwhile Anthony proceeded alone to a series of adventures on the mountains above Clyro. These included being rescued by a tractor from a ditch when he was prospecting for The Travely, a farmhouse in which Powells had lived three hundred years before.

By Sunday morning when I was feeling frail but prepared to face a convalescent day, Anne, my hostess, reported that she had a swollen throat and that mumps, subsequently confirmed, were suspected. As a result I was deputed to drive Godfrey Winn in Anne's baby Austin to have lunch at Madresfield with Lord and Lady Beauchamp. This house was full of interest for me because my grandmother had hoped that the previous Lord Beauchamp would propose to my mother. She herself quite fancied the idea as Madresfield was, she thought, a romantic grange. Lord Beauchamp did not propose, but the house-party settled my mother's fate. Lord Longford, a fellow guest and a cousin of the host, fell in love with Mary Villiers when, on the way back to London, she had sprinted like Atalanta along Swindon platform to buy a bag of buns.

Crossing the Malvern Hills and thinking of Piers Plowman, 'meetless and moneyless', I managed to stall Anne's Baby Austin on the steepest bend of Whyche Hill. We slid helplessly backward until rescued by a kind young man who diagnosed a disconnected petrol pipe. Luckily he failed to recognise Godfrey Winn who by that time had become a familiar face on television. I was, however, disconcerted to discover that when we arrived at Madresfield one of the guests had assumed that Winn and I were a married couple. I wish I had had the opportunity to disabuse her as she happened to be one of my grandmother's one hundred first cousins, although forty years younger.

My mother had a lucky escape that Madresfield did not become her home. She married my father, a professional soldier, and followed the flag until he was killed at Gallipoli in 1915. Lord Beauchamp married one of her cousins but, after thirty years and the birth of seven children, he found that leanings towards his own sex obliged him to leave the country. It is reported that he had kept a weather eye on leaving by salting away a thousand pounds in cash to finance any such sudden flitting.

My first book, *Five Out of Six*, was published in November 1960. From Dublin my sister-in-law Christine Longford wrote that the book had launched my brother Edward on a flood of reminiscence. It is a deep regret to me that I did not urge Edward to start recording his recollections, but I could not know how little time was left to him.

Born in December 1902, Edward was thirteen years old when the last hopes were given up that his father could have survived the attack on what had been called 'the terrible country round Suvla Bay'. He had spent formative years in a prosperous pre-1914 world but the loss of his father also involved a change of identity. He had been called Silchester, a second title which gave the Earls of Longford a seat in the House of Lords. His mother now announced to her younger children that Silchester was to be called Edward. I recollect her doing so to my sister Julia and me, aged respectively two and four years old. Silchester became a ship sunk with all on board. Being nine years older he was hardly a figure in the forefront of my nursery life, but I can remember the feeling that a semi-stranger was being replaced by a complete stranger.

The ten months, when there was a possibility that the Brigadier-General commanding the South Midland Mounted Brigade might have survived as a prisoner of war, established an embarrassment among his children which his wife's emotional inhibitions were powerless to disperse. I can honestly say that I can never remember Edward mentioning the name of his and my father, unless obliged to do so by estate workers or neighbours.

The flood of reminiscence, said to have been released by *Five Out of Six*, had boiled up from a past which at his marriage he had cast aside. Ireland, according to Dean Swift, may be 'no country for old men', but it is undeniably a country where fat men are less remarkable than in the rest of the British Isles. There was a huge increase in Edward's weight by the time he was thirty-seven, even by Irish standards. He had competitors among his fellow Irish peers, Lord Castlerosse, ten years older, Lord Elveden, ten years younger, but, as they say in racing circles, these were way down the course.

As the years went on, Edward and Christine spent ever more time in Dublin, time dedicated to the affairs of the Gate Theatre. Having no children of his own, Edward had never left his childhood, when he had written and produced plays at family Christmas parties. In Dublin he was rich enough to function as a patron, with wares of his own to be put into production. For thirty years both the Gate and Longford productions were mistresses who needed to be placated with continual infusions of cash.

My reflections came from remembering the February day in 1961 when Frank reported Edward as 'gravely ill'. He died on the fourth of that month unconscious from a massive stroke. By previous arrangement his nephew Thomas Pakenham, my godson, reigned in his stead.

Stricken with influenza, I could not go to Dublin for Edward's funeral, a particularly wise decision, as I had once got pneumonia from travelling back from Ireland in a fevered condition. I had heard second-hand that it was a crowded occasion, those of the Roman faith attending in the churchyard. Tristram described how a red-faced figure was seen reeling among the tombstones. This turned out to have been Brendan Behan, paying his last respects to someone who had devoted his life and fortune to promoting the theatre throughout Ireland. Emotion appeared to have overwhelmed Behan who, a day or two later, came before a magistrate with two black eyes and a charge of wilful damage and assaulting the police. Tristram also reported that he and his cousin Ferdy Mount had been invited by Lady Nugent for a day or two's shooting at Ballinlough, Co. Westmeath, because 'the woodcock were in', a rite of spring in the Irish countryside.

At home I had risen from my sickbed to entertain Laura and Evelyn Waugh who were staying down the road at Mells Manor. Edward's death had been received by Evelyn with peculiarly mixed feelings. In the years immediately after divorce from his first wife, Evelyn had led a nomadic life among the houses of his friends. At Pakenham he stayed consistently, even on one occasion importing his early love Alastair Graham. Evelyn's later metamorphosis as a member of White's Club, officer in the Blues and country squire, inclined him to distance himself from an earlier dowdier phase of his social life. This attitude became clear when the Waugh diaries and letters were published. In 1961 Evelyn showed little appreciation of his hostess's frail condition, and complained in his diary of the frivolous atmosphere in what might have been expected to have been a house of mourning.

Curiously enough, Edward and Christine, whose taste in Chinese objets d'art was well suited to the house they were refurnishing, could not be trusted with a pot of paint. Mercifully they left the bookcases in the remarkable library untouched, but they tackled the Great Hall and the dining-room with a determination to obliterate what they regarded as bogus baronialism. The hall was given an unsuitable coating of red and blue, while the panelling in the dining-room was painted a particularly harsh lime green, above which a row of rather undistinguished family portraits looked ill at ease.

Thomas, in due course, stripped the paint from the panels and restored the original setting. He also banished some solidly wooden chairs, vaguely Chinese in design, which had inflicted agonies on guests for thirty-odd years. With taste and judgement he unblocked a window in the drawing-room, said to have been built up by my grandparents to avoid beggars actually peering in on Pakenhams drinking tea.

It was a shock to my mother, coming from sedate Oxfordshire, to find that beggars presented themselves at the front door of what was locally known as 'the Castle'. In the interests of decorum, she tried to persuade supplicant tenants to present themselves at side doors, of which the house had an inordinate number. The result was that a black-shawled figure might be found on any doorstep. Requests could sometimes be satisfied in unexpected ways. A mother, seeking for 'a bit of white' to put on a child going to her first communion, gladly accepted a pair of boots, which could be traded for the white to be worn on Easter morning.

After twenty-five years in Ireland, ten of them as a widow, threatened by war at sea and on land, my mother closed that chapter of her life with an almost audible slam. Never swerving in her devotion to her eldest son, she was wise enough not to sample the Nationalist regime which he had set up, with the tricolour of the Irish Free state flying from the tower of Pakenham Hall.

3

RIDING DOWN TO PETRA

ONCE, in the 1930s, hacking home after a day with the Bicester hounds, I found myself riding beside the landlord of the Bull Hotel, Aylesbury's grandest hostelry. The innkeeper was another who had obviously escaped from a novel by R. S. Surtees. His face was near aubergine in colour, his hair had a gingery tint, and my recollection is that he wore a ratcatcher coat of mustard tweed. It was unexpected to hear this essentially sporting figure describe his visit to Petra, quoting inevitably Dean Burgeon's lines about the rose red city. Petra seemed a long way from a winter twilight in the Vale of Aylesbury.

More details about Petra came my way in the years before I actually rode down El Siq, and the glowing pink treasure was revealed. Mrs Dobbs, mother of my friend Kitty Muggeridge and youngest of the eight formidable Potter sisters, had brought back watercolours of Petra, she being a tireless outdoor sketcher. Besides a conventional study of the red cliffs, she had painted a fantasy of the rocky columns giving them, as Kitty pointed out, the likenesses of her elder sisters.

Another saga of Petra was that of Camilla Sykes, whose husband Christopher was an experienced traveller in the Middle East. He had arranged for his then fiancée, Camilla, and his twin sister to climb up to the High Place, led by a guide one of whose names was Jesus, or so Camilla said. As the two girls struggled up the rocks, the guide halted, drew a knife and approached Camilla. She said that she closed her eyes, prepared to show how an English lady could die, when she found that the thoughtful Jordanian only wanted to slit the seam of her skirt, which he had observed to be too tight for comfortable climbing.

This preamble will explain how irresistible a Swan Cruise that included Petra would be. An additional pleasure was the company of my niece, Antonia Fraser. She was due for a holiday after the birth of her third child, and had calculated that her schedule would just about fit. She had come to stay sometime before the expected birth, to the delight of Mrs Manley from our lodge who had been a district nurse. She had never lost the accent of her native Glasgow and exclaimed joyfully, 'Och, wouldn't it be grand if Lady Antonia had the baby here.' Mercifully, Benjamin delayed his arrival but it was a close thing that Antonia was able to meet us at the air terminal on a breezy April morning. We sailed from Venice, Dubrovnik being our first port of call. Leaving the main group, Antonia, Anthony, John and I decided to take a walk round the ramparts. This independent action must have aroused the suspicions of the Titoist authorities. We soon realised that we were being tailed by a diminutive Jugo-Slav of considerable age who stopped whenever we paused to admire the stunning views. He wore a curiously-shaped felt hat, a suit of checks, a poor relation of

Antonia Fraser and AP, Delos 1961

the check suit in which Evelyn Waugh prowled round his garden, and black and white co-respondent shoes on the point of disintegration. We realised that keeping us in his sight was essential to his livelihood, but it was impossible to explain that we did not expect him to admire the view. Two years later, when we again toured the battlements of Dubrovnik, surveillance had slackened and there was not a 'tail' in sight.

In the dining saloon on board the *Ankara* we shared a table with Antonia and the Antrims, Ran and Angela. John and the Antrims' son Hector ate in the dormitory mess, where they were given champagne by their mess-mates. I had known Angela since schoolroom days, when we had danced in the same minuet at a charity matinée, and Ran had belonged to the debutant world of my first London season. At our table the three other seats were occupied by a lady who taught English at a boy's public school and by an academic couple from a Californian university.

The academic husband and wife had, it turned out, some difficulty in sorting out the names of their British table-mates. One evening when the Dodecanese were silhouetted against a rosy-fingered sunset, Ran Antrim pointed out to me an island which he, as a naval officer, had liberated at the end of the Second World War. On this emotional occasion he had been presented with the classical gifts of bread and salt, but his injunction that some sort of local government should be set up, at once resulted in a split between the two villages he had liberated. Happening to find myself leaning over the rail beside the American professor from our table, I explained that the island past which we were sailing had, at the end of the last war, been liberated by Lord Antrim, his neighbour at meals. Presumably confused between Antrim, Anthony and Antonia he replied bemusedly, 'Oh, really, did she?'

On this cruise a number of more or less amorous relationships came into being, and dissolved with astonishing rapidity. When we reached Beirut, from which Petra was to be visited, these alliances were already delicately balanced. Before we left for Petra, Antonia was persuaded by the English doctor on board that the ride would be unwise so soon after her confinement, so she changed to a one-day trip to Krak des Chevaliers. Consequently it was only Anthony, John and I who flew to the desert landing-strip at Ma'an, the terminus of a railway that featured in the fighting days of T. E. Lawrence. From there a motorcade of competitive drivers jostled their way to El-Ji, a *Beau Geste* style of fort, from whence the ride to Petra began.

There was a line-up of nippy little Arab horses, guided by a single woollen rein, and battered saddles polished by the bottoms of many travellers. The Arabs themselves were keen on a quick turn-round, pleas of 'No gallop' were treated with contempt. They refused to be daunted by one gallant lady of considerable size, but she required an Arab helper on both sides to keep her in the saddle.

My horse was called Salwar and, rather against my will, his owner insisted on taking charge of my bag as, like Camilla Sykes, I was having difficulty with my skirt. The sun was low and the sudden sight of the Treasury carved out of red rocks was more ruby than rose red, only less bright than the crimson poppies that carpeted the valley. As we came out into the wadi that leads to Petra camp, the horses smelt the end of the journey and broke into a gallop. Suddenly I was aware that Salwar's owner had deserted me and was crouched on the side of the wadi, apparently rifling my bag. With horsemanship that surprised myself, I kicked Salwar round and charged towards the squatting figure. Luckily, before I had actually ridden the Arab down, I remembered that some Asiatics get down on their heels to urinate, so I quickly went into reverse.

Thirty-five years ago the camp at Petra offered a choice of tombs or tents in which to sleep. We had chosen tents but, as Antonia was a non-starter, John had a tent to himself in which he slept unperturbed for eight hours. Bedtime was early at Petra, the camp's sleep being guarded by a picturesque figure with a long antique rifle, as if in a 19th-century painting of an Arab encampment. There were a few hours of silence only broken by the oleander's whispers. Then the dogs of the Bedouins began to call each other, dog answering dog in high, mournful voices. Cocks crew, birds began their own dawn chorus, and sleep was finally banished before five o'clock by the loud hee-haw of a donkey.

When the Swiss traveller Burckhardt rediscovered Petra in 1812 he remarked on the rough-hewn figure of a camel, seated on its haunches, that brooded over the Nabatean tombs. The camel remains an indisputable image of an animal essential to the life of the inhabitants. On our visit, however, the resident archaeologist was sceptical when I suggested that at sunrise other images could be seen among the shadows of the red rocks. Suggestions from the laity are not always welcomed by professional archaeologists. I was assured that a profile curiously like Voltaire's and the full lips and swelling breasts of a young Nubian were accidents of nature, untouched by human hand. Afterwards I wondered if the prospect of opening up a new line of research might not have appalled the professional mind.

The intrepid Swan cruiser who had required the support of two Arabs when riding down to Petra was in good fettle when we boarded the aeroplane back to Beirut. She remarked cheerfully, 'The toils of the business were over, the sweets began', quoting from *Persuasion*. Sir Walter Elliot's satisfaction at becoming known to his noble kinsfolk can seldom have been quoted against a more exotic background.

Rejoining the *Ankara* we found that Antonia had abandoned the trip to Krak des Chevaliers in favour of an outing with a Lebanese playboy met at a dinner party. Hardly had we settled in the bar when a furious guest lecturer had erupted. He had mistaken Antonia's change from Petra to Krak as a personal compliment, a wish to attend his lecture on the Crusaders. He was still complaining of her cruelty years later.

The following day the ship's company visited the temples at Baalbek, and there was a long luncheon washed down with wine from vines presumably planted by the Crusaders. At that date Colonel Nasser, President of Egypt, had attempted to set up what he called the United Arab Republic, rather like a hostess who tries to create a salon but no one will patronise it. In fact only Syria had been persuaded to join this federation. Sympathy for the UAR was, however, strong at Baalbek, where Nasser's photograph flashed his teeth from many windows. In the post-luncheon doldrums, two local guides had joined our party at a purely social level (they said Antonia looked like Kim Novak) but even their chat did not finally prevent us from noticing that life had ground to a halt. Concurrently, Lebanese army carriers were seen circling the hotel.

At length Sir Mortimer Wheeler gave his talk on the Temple of Jupiter, while an armed guard protected the company from a pro-Nasser demonstration. The only sign of apprehension among the Swan group was a slight tendency to stick with their friends rather than to wander singly among the columns of the temple. The rioters, thought to have been recruited from Syria, must have had a draughty ride home. In the course of the demonstration the windows of the coaches in which they had travelled were seen to have been smashed into splinters.

A day or two later we docked in Cyprus, but Antonia and I decided to cut the day's trip, 'the work sheet' as someone called it, in favour of a bathe at the Turkish section of the island. This meant we had the pleasure of sailing on board what was practically our private yacht. The *Ankara* was not in fact entirely empty. Climbing up to the boat deck for a morning's rest in the sun, we were interested to come upon the ship's radio officer, always a powerful figure in any vessel. On this occasion an SOS would have gone unanswered, the officer responsible being locked in a clinch with a passenger who had the letters MFH after her name on the passenger list. She may have controlled the hunting field but Turkish technique had reduced her to delighted giggles.

The final pleasure of this cruise was to sit in the Piazza di San Marco and to watch our fellow passengers trailing off towards the Ferrovia, with the happy knowledge that a night in Venice was still before us. The last enjoyment of Italy could not even have been spoilt by the coach driver taking us to the wrong Milan airport. Rectifying his mistake, the driver showed skills worthy of Fangio.

4.

SUMMER'S MERRY-GO-ROUND

ONLY two weeks after the end of the cruise the American Embassy issued an invitation for a reception in the Library with, as it turned out, a suitably intellectual guest list. This was my first experience of a gathering in the new Embassy which had swept away a row of houses, some eighteenth, some nineteenth century, on the west side of Grosvenor Square.

In the years before 1939 the American occupation of this famous enclave had been, I think, limited to the United States Consulate which had its home in a large mansion on the east side. The Consul General who issued visas in the 1930s was an impressive figure who handed back passports with an almost sacramental gravity. My great aunt Mabel Leigh, herself an American from Savannah, Georgia, had been unaware of the reverence expected from applicants. Sometime in the 1920s she had been to the Consulate to collect the passport of her grown-up daughter Peggy. Aunt Mabel had a charming appearance but she married late and was already grey-haired. When the name of Margaret Ethel Leigh was called, she stepped forward and bowed politely. 'Aged eighteen?' asked the Consul in some astonishment. Aunt Mabel bowed again with the grace of a Southern belle and swept out with the passport in her hand.

Aunt Mabel, née Gordon, had married my grandfather's youngest brother Rowley Leigh after a seven-year engagement. Uncle Rowley was a spoilt, unemployed, youngest son, but an appointment as a handicapper to the Jockey Club finally made his marriage possible. They lived in what was regarded as a small house, and their means corresponded. Consequently when their daughter Peggy, who had been impersonated by her mother, was married, the house of her uncle Dudley (Duddy to his family) was the obvious place at which the reception could be held. This house, on the west side of Grosvenor Square, was among those to be obliterated by the new United States Embassy. This preamble is leading to a recollection of it and its neighbours as I knew them.

The Leighs had a drawing-room upholstered in scarlet brocade, presumably by Lord Leigh's first American wife, Helen Beckwith, a beauty who had frequented the court of Napoleon III. She had been older than my uncle Duddy, and her death was thought to have been partly due to her efforts to keep up with her remorselessly energetic husband. The marrying of Americans was engrained in the Leigh family. Fourteen years later he married another, Marie Campbell, a charming lady from New York, a number of years younger than himself, though this adjustment of the age level did not result in any children. Aunt Marie imported touches of modern luxury to her husband's houses but she could not obliterate the high Victorian décor of 31 Grosvenor Square.

The year of Peggy Leigh's wedding to Charles Graves happened to be 1929, when a ten year's silence was broken by more than one writer who had survived the horrors of World War I. These literary time-bombs caused scandal, none more so than *Goodbye to All That*, written by Robert Graves, brother of Peggy's bridegroom. Charles himself led the precarious life of a journalist, mostly gossip-writing, and he had been regarded as a rather undesirable son-in-law by Peggy's parents. When *Goodbye to All That* appeared the outrage was too widespread to be ignored, and Charles found himself in the ludicrous position of assuring his wife's family that he had never had any contact with his brother, and was himself a pattern of conventionality.

A cousin of my Aunt Mabel had married Rudyard Kipling, and Peggy had been on sisterly terms with Elsie, the Kiplings' surviving daughter. Aunt Mabel told me that there was a feeling of strain when she visited Bateman's because Kipling always wanted to talk about his son John, killed in 1916, while Mrs Kipling could not bear to have his name mentioned. The Kiplings naturally came to the reception in

Grosvenor Square, and in the crowd I suddenly found myself gazing fascinated into Kipling's eyes. Or rather I gazed into what I could see under eye-brows as beetling as the samphire on the White Cliffs of Dover. I am happy to say that we did exchange a glance, but Mrs Kipling remained abstracted, a small black tee-to-tum.

A few doors from the Leighs' house stood the mansion in which Robert Fleming had established his family. Mr Fleming bore the somewhat volatile label of the richest commoner in England. It was at the time he was in the City and he and his wife were living in an undistinguished Surrey villa that she suggested that his overcoat was looking rather worn. Unthinkingly he replied that perhaps it was a bit shabby for a millionaire. After that Mr Fleming never had a moment's peace until his family were set up in Grosvenor Square and on an Oxfordshire estate of many acres. Only once did I myself attend a party in the Flemings' imposing house, and then, for reasons long forgotten, I left by the back stairs and a door into the mews. My father-in-law, Philip Powell, had a very different experience, one which passed into family legend. As a young soldier, after a convivial night out, he found himself with a friend who was in no state to get home on his own. This friend, Robert Hermon-Hodge, happened to be married to a daughter of Robert Fleming. Captain Powell escorted Mr Hermon-Hodge back to Grosvenor Square. The doorbell was answered by a respectable figure in evening dress. Presuming this to be the butler, my father-in-law explained the Mr Hermon-Hodge (later to become Lord Wyfold) was not feeling very well, and needed help to get up to bed. He reinforced an appeal for silence on the subject by pressing half-a-crown into the hand that opened the door. Only later did he discover that he had contributed two-and-sixpence to the coffers of 'the richest commoner in England'.

The last of the private palaces of Grosvenor Square where I was entertained was probably the most palatial. It belonged to the family associated with the Tranby Croft scandal of card-cheating in the fastest Victorian racing circles. Nothing like that happened at the debutante ball which I attended, though the behaviour of a cousin of my mother's had a hint of Edwardian loucheness. Her name also happened to be Violet, and she was famous among her kindred for the pursuit of young men, finding her middle fifties no impediment. Shunning the chaperone's bench, she seated herself among what Tennyson called 'the garden of girls', complaining of the intolerably long intervals between dances. She was obviously seeking for fresh young blood on which to feed.

At the party given in May 1961 the American Embassy had trawled widely in literary and academic waters. From a distance I mistook the much-photographed Bishop of Southwark for the equally much-photographed Dr A. L. Rowse, the historian and Fellow of All Souls. Anthony, for his part, was hailed by the wave of a hand from a grey-faced figure seated with his back to the wall. This was possibly Anthony's last sight of his oldest friend Henry Yorke (Henry Green) who had, unusually, emerged from his habitual seclusion.

Then, to my pleasure, I heard my name spoken by T. S. Eliot, not seen since his marriage some years previously.

Egotistically, I was particularly glad to meet Valerie Eliot, about whom Tom wrote to Cyril Connolly, '. . . some readers were shocked that I should be so happy'. As she was distinctly younger and blonder, I hope Valerie would forgive me for mentioning that she was said to look not unlike me. I can, however, say that she has always reminded me of Manet's magnificent painting of Mademoiselle Victorine as matador, which hangs in the Metropolitan Museum of Art in New York. John Piper assured me that this picture of Manet's best-known model was always called by my name in the Piper family.

The American Embassy party was distinctly rich in literary contacts. I noted in my diary that William Cooper (Harry Hoff) was 'entertaining', without going into details. I was also told by the novelist Olivia Manning that, at a tea-party of Ivy Compton-Burnett's, my distant cousin Ivo Pakenham said that he had deliberately left the Powell coat-of-arms off the family tree which my brother Edward had commissioned him to draw up. This cousin had obviously not forgiven me for my behaviour at a party in Oxford when I had monopolised a young nobleman to whom Ivo Pakenham had taken a fancy. The fellow guests at Dame Ivy's party must have felt that they had stepped into one of her own novels.

Above the crowd Sir Mortimer Wheeler loomed, and joined us. One of his more endearing qualities was a willingness to explain the state of his heart, regardless of the audience.

On this evening he was gazing from his considerable height over the heads of the company. He had, he said, just caught sight of Professor A. J. Ayer, whose head can have barely reached Wheeler's shoulder. From information received, it was possible to gather that the philosopher and the archaeologist, the short and the tall, had been rivals for the favours of a famously beautiful girl. She had escaped them both, to marry what Wheeler disgustedly called a 'peer'.

After a glimpse of this romantic episode, Rik Wheeler came to dine with us at the Travellers Club. From a neighbouring table he was greeted with a certain amount of sardonic laughter. Rik felt obliged to explain that one of the post-cruise perils was to evade invitations to view passengers' slides. The fellow diner at the Travellers that night had sent one of these terrible invitations, only to be told by Wheeler's devoted secretary that he had once again left the country. When we came to know Rik better we found that these predicaments were endemic to his way of life.

At the beginning of June, Sonia Pitt-Rivers, widow of George Orwell, asked us to the dress rehearsal of a pageant which she was organising in aid of the churches of Cranborne Chase, the estate of her second husband Michael Pitt-Rivers. Sonia had learnt to organise in the hard school of the *Horizon* office under the editorship of Cyril Connolly. She tackled the pageant with sturdy generalship, having taken to country life with enthusiasm. This was the peak of her career as a landowner's wife.

Based on the history of Cranborne Chase, the pageant starred King John and the Duke of Monmouth. As I have written in an earlier work, the local school children were said to cry when taught that their very own king was regarded as something of a monster.

The Larmer Tree Gardens were an ideal setting for the pageant in pleasure grounds laid out by Michael Pitt-Rivers' ancestor, a general and the father of modern Archaeology. The gardens were surrounded by pavilions in different styles of architecture, mostly eastern in feeling. In spacious Victorian days, the gentry would drive in, the horses would be taken out, and refreshments would be served in the pavilions.

At the dress rehearsal, while dresses were inevitably delayed on the railway, the midges were making a meal and smokers were popular. Even without a regal outfit, Constantine Fitzgibbon was impressive as King John, striding across the grassy stage with hounds at heel. When Thomas Hardy's poem of the betrayal of King Monmouth had been read, 'rare King Monmouth' appeared from a bush looking reproachfully at the woman who betrayed him.

After the rehearsal Sonia had arranged a supper party at King John's House. This succulent meal was spiced with drama. Michael Pitt-Rivers' father, famous for awkward behaviour, had expressed disapproval of the pageant, and it was apprehended that he might make his views known by appearing like the Demon King in pantomime. This he did at the first performance, to be soothed by police officers who then persuaded him to enter one of their vehicles for his own safety.

On a two-day London season Anthony and I went to dine at the American Embassy where David and Evangeline Bruce had begun a posting which was to make their embassy the scene of so much enjoyable entertainment. Barbara Hutton, the doomed tobacco heiress, had built the house in Regent's Park, later taken over by the United States government. The three Bruce children would, it was thought, benefit by having an English tutor in the summer vacation, and my nephew Ferdy Mount was fortunate in being given the job. There was a story that the Bruce sons suffered from being deprived of immediate contact with American football, and that their tutor handled the situation by opening an account for them with the Tote. In any case, the sight of Ferdy and his charges having supper under the green light from the trees outside caused Anthony to think of Turgenev and remark 'a month in Regent's Park'.

The following day another dinner party was held in Regent's Park, at the Zoo, but in the Fellows Restaurant rather than the area fenced off for the Chimpanzees Tea Party. Bridget Parsons, fairest of her age in every sense, was the hostess, the secretary of the Zoological Society, Solly Zuckerman, having arranged that selected apes should be visited after dinner. Solly had long ago given his own chimpanzees to the Society but, as he hastened to point out, they still showed jealousy when he brought female friends to visit his former household pets. It was, however, a male member of the party who was observed to allow his hand to wander along the arm of a particularly good-looking keeper when purporting to caress the chimpanzee held by the handsome young man. Anthony was interested to see that another chimpanzee took advantage of his keeper's momentary inattention to smuggle a broom into his cage, for what purpose it was enthralling to speculate.

5

NEW BROOM AT TULLYNALLY

From Edgworthstown, on a Winter's day,
Maria to Tullynally made her way.
Crossing the bog in nervous trepidation
Close to the spot where now stands Float Station
By Coole and Turbotstown and Carne she passed
To reach Lord Longford's new built towers at last.

WHEN Maria Edgeworth made one of her many visits to her cousins at Pakenham Hall, House or Castle, as Tullynally was then variously called, it was to inspect the improvements made by the 2nd Earl of Longford. The architect Francis Johnston, whose work was remarkable for grace and simplicity, had extended the original Georgian building to something approaching the castellated 'little town' known to later generations.

Miss Edgeworth approved of what she called Lord Longford's nest and wished he might find a bird to share it. Lord Longford did so, and the nest filled rapidly with ten children. One of the three daughters, the eldest, married 'the lord of Burghley House by Stamford Town'. Edward Michael, the eldest son, built more onto his house but he never married and was succeeded by his next brother, a general. Of the younger brothers, one became an admiral, one took Anglican orders, and one, converting to Rome, was beatified as Father Paul Mary Pakenham, a Passionist monk. Another retreated to the Wicklow Mountains where he lived under the name of Parker; and the youngest, a diplomat, became minister to the Court of Sweden.

The nest must have been full to overflowing but the next generation, that of my grandparents, only produced half the number, though my parents raised the record to six. Then, as I have said, there was a genealogical cul-de-sac, the forty-six childless years of Edward and Christine. The view down the park had become yellow with ragwort, which seemed in some way symbolical of the emptiness within the house itself.

On taking up his inheritance, Thomas, my godson, filled his new home to bursting point. His hospitality was all the more enterprising because his uncle Edward, to discourage self-invited guests, had sold a number of beds. This effort at economy rebounded on Edward himself, when he found that he needed to house Longford Productions when on tour in Castlepollard.

Thomas had inherited Pakenham Hall in February 1961. By August, when we arrived, he had not only reverted to the house's ancient name of Tullynally (the Hill of the White Swan) but had dispersed the cloud of emptiness which had hung over the house for so many years. Beds had been mustered to sleep parents, two brothers, an uncle, an aunt, and Father D'Arcy SJ. Of other arrangements I particularly appreciated that a painting by Buckner of my grandmother Selina Rice-Trevor and her sister Elianore had been rescued from obscurity in the dining-room, and given an honourable place over the drawing-room fireplace. Richard Buckner, though derided by George du Maurier in *Trilby*, was a popular painter of attractive portraits. He made a name for himself in Rome, where he had painted the two Miss Rice-Trevors as *contadine* seated beside a well head.

The Irish Georgian Society, which owed its birth and prosperity to Desmond Guinness, had decided to stage a Georgian Cricket Match at Malahide Castle, since the fifteenth century home of the Talbot family. The Tullynally house-party was transported in two cars which meant that my nephew Kevin travelled curled up on my knee. Anthony flatly refused to umpire the match. He had last taken part in a game of cricket fifty years earlier and had no wish to reconnect himself. Finally umpiring was shared between my brother Frank, wearing a blue turban, and Father D'Arcy, wrapped in a cloak, his head crowned by a tall silk hat. Desmond Guinness, promoter of the match, was wearing a scarlet tunic. From this it will be clear that Georgian dress had been rather loosely interpreted. Miss Rose Talbot, sister of Lord Talbot of Malahide, was more conditioned to an Irish August and sensibly stuck to tweeds and a mackintosh. This gathering must have been one of the last when, under its wonderful beamed roof, Malahide's Great Hall was to be filled with friends. Only too soon death duties, implacable in their ferocity, drove out the Talbots.

At Tullynally Edward and Christine were only found to be separated when Edward resorted to the billiard room, but only once did Christine reveal her true feeling about her married home. When asked if she really liked so imposing a house, she said that she was obliged to like it. In some question-and-answer game, however, it became clear that it was not only the size of Tullynally that she found hard to bear. Asked the size of her ideal house, Christine snapped, 'eight rooms including lavatories'. Pressed as to whether these might include a billiard room, her answer was a poignant negative.

Edward, on the other hand, found relaxation in a game in which the power of his arm was backed by a weight suspected to be at least eighteen stone, which not infrequently drove the ball to bounce onto the floor. His only delicacy of approach was when he had an excuse to use the long cue. 'Matches have been lost by neglecting to chalk the long cue,' he would sapiently remark. I would value Steve Davis's opinion on the subject. The game being played was usually the variant of snooker without the frame of red balls known as 'slosh.'

By degrees the first wave of Thomas's house-party at Tullynally receded, and Anthony and I moved into the bedroom which had been inhabited by Edward and Christine. Thomas, still a bachelor, had not tried sleeping in their *letto matrimoniale*, an experience likened to adhering to an elephant's back. 'No wonder they had no children,' a guest complained, finding the elephant's spine an obstacle to embracement.

The room in which this awkward bed was housed had a rather peculiar shape owing to my mother's desire for privacy. As a bride she found the plumbing in her new home to be, by her standards, almost non-existent. She ordained that a slice should be cut off the large bay-windowed bedroom, and in this narrow wedge a bathroom and a lavatory were installed. The adaptation meant that a sort of vestibule was created, increasing my mother's sense of privacy; I have written elsewhere that this sense made its own rules. Travelling by herself on the last coach of the Orient Express as it approached Istanbul, she was discomposed to find that, owing to frontier complications, a Greek and Turkish sentry was posted at each end of the corridor. My mother summoned the *chef du train* and insisted that she could not tolerate such blockage of access to both lavatories. Lesser spirits would have found this protest far more embarrassing than brushing past a Greek or Turk on the way to her objective. I have always cherished a wistful hope that the Greek sentry might have been a kilted Evzone with pompoms on his toes.

Although he had decided against calling himself by the courtesy title of Silchester, Thomas kept the connection by painting the name on his motor boat. His former tutor at Magdalen, Oxford, Carl Leyser, had joined the party, and the four of us, Silchester trailing behind, drove to Athlone. Thomas wanted to take his boat down the Shannon, to the burial ground at Clonmacnois, where the clan of Con lies buried.

The foreshore of the Shannon, longest river in the British Isles, was unattractively littered with the corpses of eels, and the refined hotel refused to sell Guinness in the lounge. It was a relief to reach Clonmacnois, described by T. W. Rolleston as 'St Kieran's city fair … where many a blue eye of Clan Con the turf covers, many a swan-like breast.' Anthony drove one of Thomas's motor cars to the burial ground, but Carl travelled by boat with Thomas. The romance of Rolleston's rendering of the Irish of Angus O'Gillan was, I hope, compensation for the soaking of Carl's cavalry twill trousers when he and Thomas struggled ashore.

Equally romantic but more sinister were the graves of Tristernagh, seat of the baronet who was the villain of John Betjeman's poem, 'Sir John Piers'. I think it was probably on one of his many visits to Tullynally that the Poet Laureate came across *Annals of Westmeath, Ancient and Modern*, by James Woods. This was to be the source of one of Betjeman's most brilliant narrative poems, a tale of brutal seduction, followed by the revenge of Fate and the seducer's ruin.

At a fête-champêtre on Lough Ennel, Co. Westmeath, Sir John Piers begins his assault on Lady Cloncurry. Her husband was Lord Cloncurry, the patriot, whose opposition to the Act of Union had earned him two years in the Tower of London. Sir John Piers was one of his intimate circle, but this had not prevented the baronet from betting a large sum that he could break up the Cloncurrys' marriage. Had Sir John failed the sum would have been forfeited, but he did not fail. A sensational trial for crim. con. (adultery) followed which resulted in heavy damages. Sir John Piers fled to the Isle of Man, later returning to Tristernagh where he barricaded himself with a wall 'against the vista and the duns'.

Divorced by an Act of Parliament in 1807, Lord Cloncurry married four days afterwards. In 1819 Lady Cloncurry herself remarried what must have been a distinctly broadminded clergyman from Somerset. Sir John Piers was indisputably the all-round loser, his wager being absorbed by the damages which the law exacted, and in Betjeman's words his 'old delight by other lips is tasted'. This extremely moral tale had no lasting effect on behaviour in Co. Westmeath. A hundred and twenty years later a string of divorces resulted in a gale of laughter at anyone who admitted belonging to the county of marital free-for-all.

As a letter of thanks I sent Thomas some verses, the first of which is quoted at the beginning of this chapter. The last verse ran:

> Maria's bones long since are lapped in earth,
> But Tullynally's walls still ring with mirth
> Beauty and wit exert their ancient spell
> Tho' Wits of beauties sometimes cruelties tell
> But all salute in grateful unison
> Thomas dear host of sixty-one.

6.

TAKINGS OFF

THROUGHOUT The Chantry the fireplaces follow a Regency pattern, decreasing in the upper floors, but even in the attics retaining a hint of classicism. The exception was the dining-room where someone devoid of any sense of elegance had installed a carved oak monstrosity which looked even less appealing when we had it painted white. Anthony stuck a knife down the back of the mantelshelf and it seemed possible that there was something more than a black hole behind. To general delight, a charming white marble surround inset with mottled grey was revealed.

Painters were in the house and at that moment asked what colour we wished the two alcoves, features of the dining-room, to be painted. These alcoves were the homes for two busts, Caracalla, 'enemy of mankind', and Antinous, the lover of Hadrian. Originally they had been part of a group which Wyndham Ketton-Cremer had found in the attics of his magnificent house, Felbrigg, near Cromer. Wyndham had offered them to us in return for a donation to a local fête and the price of the petrol to his agent who had offered to drive them down from Norfolk. The busts travelled in style, displaying their classical features to astonished passing drivers from the windows of a Land Rover.

Without specifying the exact shade of grey, I indicated to the painters that they should copy the marble surround. With unforeseen brilliance the painters achieved a subtle mottled grey effect. Their skill impressed John Piper, himself a painter in many a medium, to such a degree that he could only wish he had such workmen to fulfil his designs at the Royal Opera House, Covent Garden.

Over the newly revealed elegance of the fireplace we hung the Augustus John drawing in sanguine of Anthony. This had been completed in the previous year, but it had been difficult to get it released, the sitter being highly sympathetic to the painter. Finally I went on a foray, and returned in triumph after a session with Augustus that had its comic dénouement. From the drawings propped up in the room in which he had worked on Anthony, Augustus indicated an undeniably chocolate-boxy picture of a girl. The sitter, he wryly explained, had never turned up to collect what had been intended to be a present. I was wondering if this pretty girl had felt that the price might be too high, when a girl—not the subject of the drawing—came into the room. Most respectfully she asked if she might take a glass of the sherry which Augustus and I had been drinking. It was needed, she explained, for the dish which Dorelia was cooking for luncheon. Augustus agreed, genially, and I enquired if that were a daughter-in-law. 'Something of the sort,' growled Augustus, suggesting a category that might be said to cover a multitude of sins.

The drawing of Anthony was a remarkable success but his alert gaze was objected to by Henry Bath, sitting on my right hand at dinner. When Gerry Wellington invited himself for the night on his way to a family wedding, I rang to invite the Baths to dinner, adding that Henry would not have to sit opposite the Augustus drawing. 'Somerset?' inquired Henry, referring to a ducal neighbour and friend. 'Wellington,' I snapped back.

Gerry had a distinct fondness for what an earlier generation would have called risqué jokes. When he wrote in his letter of thanks that he was happy to find that he could still blush, we felt that the party had been a success. As far as I could make out, the conversation that had raised a blush to Gerry's cheeks concerned a recent incident at the Baths' house, Job's Mill. An ambassador, with his wife, had been invited to open a charity show at Longleat, and to stay the night. When they realised that the night would be spent in the charming but restricted Job's Mill rather than at Longleat, it became clear that their feelings were those of guests at a five-star hotel who find themselves relegated to the annexe. Not only was the ambassadorial pair deprived of a night in a top stately home, but they were given only one bedroom for themselves, though their marriage was rumoured to exist on the most distant terms. Henry, having reason to get up in the small hours, reported that the light had been on in the visitors' bedroom. However he interpreted this, he might have been amused that, pausing to call on a former Prime Minister, the ambassador sent his wife back to London by train.

Although only five volumes of *Dance* had appeared by 1961, what might be called a coven of addicts had built up on the East Coast of the United States. This resulted in an invitation for Anthony to do a round of colleges—Dartmouth, Amherst, Cornell, together with a publisher's gala in New York City. The visa for this expedition was issued by a young lady who had been over-schooled to approach her work unpompously. After expressing surprise that his newspaper employers could spare him for so many days, she was defeated by the 'object of the visit'. The description that she finally chose—Informal talks to Ivy League Colleges—provoked mirthful incredulity when shown to Anthony's hosts.

Following a successful post-ing in Japan, Mary and Lees Mayall, our dear friends and neighbours, were *en poste* for Lisbon, which for parents of school-age children, seemed advantageous geographically. They had welcomed my sug-gestion of a visit, but before I set off I had agreed to be interviewed for *Queen* magazine on the subject of 'What I feel about Christmas'. This involved being photographed by John Hedgecoe, then at the beginning of his career. He posed me under a tree in

the garden of the Curzon House Club, and over coffee discoursed on gossip from the *Queen* office. I found this rivetting as Tristram had been a *Queen* employee, though I occasionally bleated, 'Are you sure that you ought to be telling me all this?' The result of this session was that I got star billing and a big picture, in which I gazed heavenwards with a soulful expression. The others photographed in the Christmas feature were given smaller pictures, though they were undeniably better known than myself: 'Giles', Osbert Lancaster (both artists on the *Daily Express*), John Betjeman, not yet Poet Laureate, and Lady Dartmouth, subsequently Lady Spencer and still later the Comtesse de Chambrun, who showed the Christmas spirit by wearing a tiara for her photograph.

It was twenty-six years since Anthony and I had spent a holiday in Lisbon, travelling by a Dutch boat to a city that was not yet a base for spies and the refuge of exiled royalty. We had spent some time at Mont'Estoril where a cluster of mostly male couples in the adjoining villages of Cascais and Estoril were seeking escape from moral or financial difficulties. Certain rivalries existed among these pairs of friends, as we found when our host for luncheon was discovered, by someone uninvited, buying *foie gras* for our entertainment.

In return for various hospitality, we gave a party on the broken-down terrace of the casino at Cascais. As well as our somewhat louche friends, we invited two English couples whose basic respectability did not prevent them from taking a keen interest in the ex-patriots. One of the wives hissed in my ear, 'Is he a relation of . . . ?', to which I cruelly replied, 'He is a relation of nobody,' not however adding that he had been found by his present protector in a Turkish bath.

In 1964 the flat, to which Lees Mayall's position as counsellor entitled him, was an apartment from whose terrace the shipping on the Tagus could be observed. This was an endlessly fascinating view, particularly on the Sunday in spring when the fishing fleet, duly blessed and dressed overall, sailed for the Grand Banks and a season's cod fishing. To those brought up on Kipling's *Captains Courageous* the sight was as moving as that of men going off to war. In the film version of *Captains Courageous*, Manuel, the Portuguese hand on board the *We're Here* had been played by Spencer Tracy, turned into the hero who regenerates Harvey, played by Freddie Bartholomew. The charming boy took on the persona of Kipling, and we were amused to see, when having lunch with his Aunt Cissie, that Freddie was required to autograph copies of the *Grand Banks*.

Dried cod is a staple of Portuguese diet but fresh food comes in daily. In the morning, fisherwomen would patter past my bedroom window, the baskets on their heads just visible above the shutters. This was a delightful change after early morning in the Curzon House Club when the squad of cleaners for the MI5 office opposite would come tramping up from the tube station. The leader may have had security clearance but she urged her fellows up the hill with a voice that shattered brass.

By way of an introduction Mary Mayall and I drove to call on the palace of Bacalhoa (Cod Castle) whose conical towers overlooked a short canal designed, we were told, for boat trips. The trips must have been unadventurous but the walls were prettily decorated with coloured tiles peculiar to Portugal. When we arrived, the granddaughter of the American chatelaine was riding a magnificent stallion round the forecourt. This black-haired beauty was said to have the entrée to bull-fighting society from whence came the horse she was exercising.

The Portuguese, I believe, claim that their bull fights are more classical than the Spanish, and picadors do not incite the bull to charge inferior horses. A rider, dressed as it might be bad 'Sir Jasper' in an old-fashioned melodrama, circles the ring on a horse in splendid condition. It was on one of these horses that the beauty of Bacalhoa was circling the forecourt.

Four years later Anthony and I were taken to a bookshop in Salisbury, Connecticut, satisfyingly stacked with books, and pervaded with a slight air of mystery without which a bookshop cannot be called distinguished. There was also a slight air of mystery about the proprietor, who was rumoured to be of Slav origin but to have married a wife of impeccable New England background. Suddenly, hearing his name, I realised that he was the father of the young horsewoman of Bacalhoa. She could be said to have passed by lineage from Edith

Wharton, by way of Dostoievsky to Ernest Hemingway. Any novelist would have flinched at including such a far-fetched coincidence.

Although when Anthony returned from 'informal talks to Ivy League Colleges' he fell asleep after breakfast for three consecutive days, he had recovered by the day of Augustus John's funeral at Fordingbridge. Typically of the John family, no time appeared to have been set for the ceremony. When we reached the church some time before eleven, we found a group of villagers, almost consciously Hardyesque in appearance, clustered outside. They assured us that some mourners had arrived at ten o'clock, only to go away disappointed.

To fill in time we strolled through the village and it was natural that snapshots of Augustus' last years should flash across the inward eye. On one of our last visits we had gone with the master to inspect what was to be his final large painting, illustrating a legend of the Camargue, called the Trois Maries.

The fact that one Marie was a very dark-skinned gypsy recalled the preoccupation of Augustus' early years. About twenty years earlier, a 'modern' studio had been built in the grounds at Fryern, designed on two storeys, the lower floor intended for picture storage. This plan was hardly a success, mice attacking the stored pictures to such a degree that they needed to be trimmed before sale. Neither did the studio appeal to the artist. Consequently it was to his black tarred out-building in the garden that we went to inspect the Trois Maries. Throughout our visit Augustus grumbled that he was held up in his painting because he had no model. Soon afterwards he wrote to me complaining that I had let him down. I then realised that he had hoped that I might volunteer to pose as one of the Trois Maries. All other considerations apart, my vanity would not have been strong enough to compensate for the long haul to Fordingbridge.

Returning to the day of the funeral, we realized that matters were becoming serious when a Royal Navy helicopter buzzed overhead bringing Admiral Sir Caspar John, First Sea Lord, back from a mission to Pakistan for his father's funeral. When the church filled up, the family processed up the aisle, Dorelia uniquely wonderful to look at, supported by her son Romilly, and her stepson the Admiral. Poppet and

Vivien followed, each superb in their individual looks, after which, like a diminishing shoal of fish, the procession dwindled. Taking the service, the incumbent was obviously enjoying a full house and a distinguished congregation, both possibly rare in his experience. In his address he chose to quote 'I hope to see my pilot face to face when I have crossed the bar.' This line, always difficult to work out—the pilot appearing to be going the wrong way— produced suppressed giggles, even more difficult to suppress when reminded of the Almighty's assurance, 'at my right hand are pleasures evermore.' It would be reasonable to assume that the Trois Maries would be there to welcome Augustus whatever his destination.

On our way home Sonia Pitt-Rivers gave us a reviving luncheon, and two weeks later Sonia and Michael came to dinner, bringing Caroline Blackwood and her then husband Israel Citkowitz. The Lancasters were staying with us, also my nephew Thomas Pakenham. Caroline was not yet a writer but, as Thomas said, like 'the young woman of the tribe', she sat on the hearth rug and embarked on the saga of Barbara Skelton.

Finding herself a job as a dental nurse, Barbara had developed a passion for her employer. He, we were told, was a dedicated man with no interest in Miss Skelton beyond requesting her to pass him the tools of his trade. Maddened by being ignored, Barbara tried to attract his attention by handing the dentist the wrong forceps. His only reaction was 'Miss Skelton, you have no sense of spatial content.' Finally, in despair, Barbara poured boiling water over the treasured moulds, wrecking the lives of dental patients, and then threw the burrs, the heads of drills, into the garbage can. Not surprisingly, Caroline said, 'Helty Skelty', as she was called in New York, found herself seeking other employment. As Karen Lancaster remarked, it was a myth-making evening.

And on November 27th Anthony finished *The Kindly Ones* which at once became my favourite volume in *A Dance to the Music of Time*, never losing its place in my affections.

7

THE SNOWY YEARS 1962-63

The Kindly Ones, finished thirteen months before, finally appeared to applause in December 1962, sandwiched between Anthony's 57th birthday and the Feast of Christmas. The year had come in with a snowfall that was inconvenient, particularly when thawing. The Old Year, however, reserved its Spectacular for its going out. This may be best described by a poem of Dunsany's written thirty years before when Co. Meath had been buried by a blizzard.

> A black horse came to visit us,
> We heard his hoof-beats drumming,
> All the way from the frozen east.
> He was three days coming,
> And on his back was a lady white,
> So cruelly did she ride him
> That he dropped at our doors one night
> When she softly stepped from astride him.

To those accustomed to the Mendips in winter a light snowfall is disregarded, but some prevision warned us that it might be unwise to attempt a party that Isabel and Michael Briggs were giving in their fascinating Gothic castle.

I had first known Midford Castle as derelict when I had driven Cyril Connolly over to inspect a folly, built indeed by a Connolly, but one thought to be no relation of Cyril. The castle's shape, an ace of clubs, was said to celebrate the turn of card on which the builder had won a fortune. True or not, the house was perfectly sited on one of the volcanic valleys that surround the hot springs of Bath.

On the occasion of my visit with Cyril, Deirdre Craven, as she then was, came too. Her car stuck on a steep muddy drive-way, Cyril gallantly pushing it up hill. In the face of sneers from friends, I insisted that such an energetic display of helpfulness could only lead to marriage which, sure enough, it did. I mention this to show that I was aware that Midford Castle stood on a road almost perpendicular.

A couple of days into 1963, news of the Briggs's party percolated to Chantry. Isabel Colegate is a novelist of great ability but she might have hesitated to embody that evening's drama in fiction. Henry Bath, with his wife Virginia and his son Christopher, had left the party at a prudently early hour. Henry had just congratulated himself that he had surmounted the last hazard, a hill called appropriately Black Dog, when he crashed into a car that had been abandoned in a snowdrift. The party struggled to the nearest cottage like characters in a fairy story. Leaving modesty on one side, Henry banged on the door, shouting 'I am the Marquess of Bath, I am stuck in a snowdrift. Please let me in.' With a new insight into the hardships of cottage life, the three of them spent the night, teeth chattering, over the dead embers of a kitchen fire.

Another party of guests set off up Midford Hill, only to return with the driver spattered with his own blood and his car embedded in a ditch. It was said that all joined in washing-up squads. Finally the hostess left a note on the kitchen table that summed up the situation: 'I think we shall be seventeen for breakfast. I Briggs.'

At Chantry isolation set in. It was three weeks before the drive was open to wheeled traffic, and then only after an appeal to the Council to send a snow plough. The door in the churchyard wall was wedged open by snow, the air was so purified that Tristram took a photograph which showed the view through both our dining-room windows and out onto Bangle Farm on the other side of the valley.

John's return to Eton was delayed by frozen pipes at Hawtrey House (Cruso's). Instead he asked his contemporary Harry Frere to stay. As it happened, Harry's father was also Anthony's publisher, whose elder son Toby, subsequently an admiral, had taken part in Tristram's film production of *See How They Run*. This enterprise had kept fifth formers at Cruso's occupied for several months, and led to Jonathan Cecil's career in the theatre.

When Harry in his mini arrived it was rather like the first sight of a sail on a desert island. He set off with John to return to his home in Kent, watched by Anthony and me with some trepidation. A mid-day telephone call did nothing to calm my nerves, but this turned out to be an invitation to dine by the then Camilla and Jeremy Fry, to meet the then Princess Margaret and Tony Snowdon.

The Frys lived on Widcombe Hill, with a romantic view over the city of Bath, dismissed, as readers of *Northanger Abbey* will remember, by Catherine Morland as unworthy of the attention of any serious painter in watercolours. Widcombe Manor had belonged to Horace Annesley Vachell, author of many books and plays.

The first success of Vachell's long life had been *The Hill*, a school story for grown-ups, about his own days at Harrow. Early in the book a new boy is taken for a first sight of Harrow by, as it happened, an Old Etonian prep school master. The boy is impressed, and his escort is so struck by the place that he declares, most improbably, 'I wish Eton had been built on a hill.' I note this as an improbability because Lees Mayall's father, an Eton housemaster known as 'Monkey' Mayall, took an opposite view of Harrow, the Hill and its school. Much depressed at the thought of the beginning of a new half at Eton, Mayall and two colleagues went over to Harrow 'and had a good laugh'.

Among the many embellishments that H. A. Vachell made to Widcombe, the most striking may well have been an imposing fountain imported from Italy. On the snowbound evening of the Frys' dinner party, a glacier of icicles hung from the top of the fountain. Every window of the house appeared to be lit up and uncurtained, as might be the backdrop of the scene from *commedia dell'arte* in silhouette, with guests preparing for dinner and the host gesticulating on the telephone. Hosts and guests have long since gone their separate ways, but in memory Widcombe Manor under snow remains A Midwinter Night's Dream.

The year 1963 continued to be marked by extremes of climate, violence, scandal and tragedy, and indeed by drama in the strictly theatrical sense. Violence began on a visit to Somerhill when a call from the Frome Police told us that our house had been broken into. The visit came to an abrupt end and we returned to the squalor that a burglary brings with it. At it happens, these burglars were brought to justice by means of a small boy whose knowledge of motor-cars and their dates was instrumental in identifying the vehicle owned by the culprits. We gave the small boy a copy of Kingsley's *The Heroes* as suitable encouragement for his acuteness.

I do not propose to enlarge on the political scandal which may have contributed to the fall of the Macmillan government. For nearly forty years the media have dug up this bone which by any standard of fair play should long since have remained decently buried.

Throughout the summer, dramatisation of *Afternoon Men* moved from a possibility to a reality. The adaptation by Riccardo Aragno, who had sharpened up the film *Divorce, Italian Style*, was finally given a month's run at the Arts Theatre Club. The theme—boy sees girl, boy can't get girl, boy finally loses girl—was played by a talented cast which included Georgina Ward, as Susan, a will-o'-the wisp heroine; James Fox, Atwater, her unsuccessful suitor; Alan Howard, drunken Fotheringham; Peter Bowles, Pringle, a literary layabout; and Jeremy Kemp as the painter Barlow. Long afterwards the production was described in all seriousness as a 'watershed'. Harold Pinter is reported to have remarked, à propos of the first production of *The Birthday Party*, that there is nothing between a two weeks flop and a classic. *Afternoon Men* had certainly not undergone a period of consolidation.

We missed the first night of *Afternoon Men* because we were booked on a Swan cruise. The *Ankara* sailed from Venice where we were to meet Ivan Morris, a professor of Japanese literature, and his wife Ayako. Ivan's kinswoman, Peggy Guggenheim, with whom the Morrises were staying, owned the most enviable dwelling, the Palazzo dei Leoni. In this white marble bungalow was housed her superb collection of contemporary art, and a pack of Tibetan terriers. Mrs Guggenheim also owned a private gondola, by then a rarity. The Tibetan hounds delighted in this privilege, one of them having recently jumped aboard with such enthusiasm that he had to be rescued from the waters of the Grand Canal.

Yakki Morris, a Japanese beauty, frequently wore western clothes. The disguise was so complete that, when she added a sun hat and dark spectacles, one of the Greek guides greeted her as our supposed daughter. This was after we had joined the *Ankara* where shipmates included Gladwyn and Cynthia Jebb (by then Lord and Lady Gladwyn), Patrick Gordon Walker, then Foreign Secretary, and his wife Audrey, Colin Anderson with his wife Morna and his daughter Rose.

Colin Anderson was an old acquaintance of Anthony's from the days of the Eton Society of the Arts. He had gone on to make a discriminating collection of pictures, of which Holman Hunt's *The Awakening Conscience* was perhaps the best known. The picture shows a spiritual crisis of a girl wearing a loose dressing gown who has been sitting on the knee of her protector while he strums on the piano. She has leapt to her feet when he makes the mistake of playing 'Oft in the stilly night'. Loose the girl's gown may be, but it is difficult not to feel that nights are going to be stiller in the future.

Maurice Bowra, the doyen of the guest lecturers, the Morrises, Anthony and I established a right to a particular sofa beside the dancing-floor, which, as at school, was bagged after dinner by whoever reached it first. It was the summer of the Twist, and whenever the band played the first notes, the 'Young Ones', of which there was a troop, took to the floor. The technique of the Twist has been described as rubbing a bath towel across one's bottom while stubbing out a cigarette end with one's left heel. The 'Young Ones' went weaving and bobbing round the dance floor in an abandon that ceased when the band changed to more sedate tunes.

Sir Maurice was to join the cruise at Olympia after a visit to Joan and Paddy Leigh Fermor's house in the Mani. Anthony had heard him lecture in the museum at Olympia in 1960. It had been a spellbinding occasion, and I assured both the Gladwyns and Sir William and Iris Hayter that they might expect a rare treat. 'Maurice at Olympia,' I said, 'is the ultimate in classical understanding.'

The *Ankara* docked at Katakolo and the ship's company were ferried by coach to a hanger-like restaurant at Olympia. As I came through the door, I heard a bellow of 'Violet! Violet!'. Maurice was seated at the end of a long table, crimson in the face and glistening with sweat. The former Vice Chancellor's lecture on the temple of Apollo, and the fight between lapis and centaurs, was given in an alcoholic haze from which sentences of brilliance emerged at intervals. The fireworks promised to the Gladwyns and the Hayters was something of a damp squib.

On the last night of a Swan cruise a gala dinner and tombola was customary. Maurice decided that he would celebrate by waltzing with me to the tune of the 'Blue Danube'. His technique on the dance floor was like that of a pony trying to break out of its stall, made no easier by his head being at the level of my shoulder. But I am proud to say that the applause, as we stamped round the floor, was a tumultuous tribute to Maurice's popularity as a lecturer, even if our dancing was more of a polka than a waltz.

In September a tragedy that darkened the last months of 1963 hit the Goldsmid family, a blow from which they might be said never to have recovered. Sarah Goldsmid, fascinatingly attractive, gifted in intellect and sport, was drowned in a boating accident off Fairlight in Sussex, together with David Winn, the cherished only son of his parents. Harry and Rosie had the support of their surviving daughter Chloe and pleasure in their grandchildren, but, as Isaiah Berlin said in his eulogy at Harry Goldsmid's memorial service thirteen years later, it was a wound that time was powerless to heal. No one in the congregation of friends that packed the synagogue would have disagreed.

One of my last diary entries for 1963 describes a scene which had a balletic quality rare in the political world. At tea at Mells with Katherine Asquith, she happened to talk about the fencing lessons which she had once shared with Venetia Montagu. Their practice took place in the garden of No. 10 Downing Street, Katharine's father-in-law, Herbert Asquith, being at that time Prime Minister. Venetia Montagu is famous as the young girl to whom Asquith wrote passionate letters, many of them composed at Cabinet meetings.

Next door, at No. 11 Downing Street, Lloyd George, then Chancellor of the Exchequer, while shaving, watched as the two beauties raised their foils in salute. Safety razors were barely invented, so it is probable that Lloyd George was using the old-fashioned cut-throat. Given his temperament, it was a miracle the future Prime Minister did not cut his throat.

8.

JAUNTS AND JOLLITIES

OUR TRAVELS during 1964 were to include my return to a career in sketching and to cover visits to three continents. These were preceded by two contrasting social occasions. Antony Hornby, of whom I have written earlier as the wisest of stockbrokers, gave a dinner for his sixtieth birthday. This was held at the Berkeley which still faced the Ritz across the main stream of Piccadilly. Before marriage I had much frequented the Berkeley and I had given my own 21st birthday party there. I can no longer remember what explanation I gave to my mother for leaving the house in a new pink outfit topped with a spray of pink orchids. She would have been unsympathetic towards such an extravagance of entertainment. In fact the Berkeley management gave me a birthday cake and the whole party cost me less than twenty pounds which, for a top London hotel, does not seem exorbitant.

Antony's birthday party was given in what was known as the 'little room', presided over by Louis, who himself was of minute stature. It also had the advantage that, on an ordinary night, evening dress was not obligatory. Antony's hospitality was fabulous, beginning with two helpings of caviar, with food and drink to follow on a similar level. At one moment I happened to be sitting next to the host when he was settling the question of the tip. It was his sixtieth birthday, Antony said, so he would be happy to make the gratuity £60.

As it happened, I remembered that Somerset Maugham had ended his novel *Theatre* in the little room at the Berkeley, when a leading actress breaks her dietary rules with a steak and chips. I do not remember if it was this that brought Mr Maugham's name into the conversation at dinner, but one of my neighbours began to pontificate on the subject of Maugham's private life. This fellow guest remarked that Maugham had had an illegitimate child by Rebecca West. A more sensible person would have said, 'Oh, really? What makes you think so?' I snapped back, 'You're thinking of H. G. Wells.' Unabashed, my neighbour continued, 'Well, anyway, he was practically a Nazi during the last War. Wearily, I replied, 'You're thinking of P. G. Wodehouse.'

We then moved on to a discussion of Mr Maugham's homosexuality which, I was assured, had developed from a *coup de foudre* late in life. A solicitor, speaking with authority, produced a dictum to silence my protest. Far from shutting up, I replied, accurately, that this solicitor, a friend of mine in early life, was talking through his hat. I am ashamed to say that I did not accept graciously a subsequent apology that was offered to me. 'That's quite all right,' I said loftily, 'I knew what I was talking about and you did not.' As literary conversations go, it would be hard to find one at a lower level.

On our recent Swan Cruise, Maurice Bowra, Warden of Wadham, had invited us to visit in February, so that Anthony could go as his guest to the Dorothy Dinner, a festival celebrating a benefactress of the college. There was a proviso attached to the invitation that I should look after myself on Saturday night. I had never been a member of the university, but I had done almost everything else in Oxford, including having a baby in the Acland Nursing Home. I felt that a Saturday's evening entertainment would not be difficult.

In Venice the previous summer Aline Berlin had suggested getting in touch when next in Oxford. This I did, and Aline hospitably replied that, though she was taking her son to *Aida*, Isaiah would be happy to entertain me. This plan developed into a dinner-party at the 17th century mansion of John Foster, Q.C. The host was searching for a spare man for a party described as of 'assorted Rothschilds'. He was prepared to accept a party of three—myself, Isaiah and Hugh Trevor-Roper, as Lord Dacre of Glanton then was—if he could gain an extra male guest.

John Foster's house was about ten miles from the centre of Oxford, and at one point the way was barred by a toll-gate. My childhood winters had been spent in Oxfordshire, and when Hugh wound down the window of his imposing Bentley I not only got a whiff of the familiar dank air but recognised the local accent and the unalert mind of the toll-gate keeper. Could he, inquired Hugh, take a return ticket? 'Oh no, Sir,' said the toll-gate keeper, speaking with the voice of a Shakespearian clown, 'you might drive into the ditch on the way back.' I doubt if Hugh, Regius Professor of History, or Isaiah, Fellow of All Souls, could have worked out the philosophical implications of this refusal.

We drove further and it became clear that we must ask where John Foster's house was to be found. Hugh again wound down the window and asked a passing villager, 'Can you tell me the way to Sir John Foster's house?' 'John Foster? You mean Jarge Foster,' was the reply, difficult to convey in writing. We did eventually arrive at the Jacobean mansion where every window was encouragingly illuminated.

In the front hall a dinner table for fourteen was laid, rather in the manner of an old-fashioned Aldwych farce when the action was apt to take place in a 'lounge hall'. We stood in a row before the fireplace waiting for the host to appear. Almost at once the front door opened and a chauffeur carrying a suitcase came marching in. Without pausing he strode through the hall and up the rather grand staircase. He was followed by a good-looking red-headed lady wrapped in furs. Like the chauffeur she ignored the three standing before the fireplace, while we turned our heads to watch the little procession in the manner of those watching Wimbledon.

It should be explained that Sir John—locally Judge Foster—was a bachelor with a great liking for attractive females. He was also an abstainer from alcohol, which is sometimes the practice of those who conduct many love-affairs. On this occasion, however, there were drinks before dinner. I came to the conclusion that the meal itself had been garnered from the deep freeze of the local Post Office. It would be fair to say that it was recognisable as food, but only by some exercise of the imagination. Mrs Miriam Lane, a famous expert on fleas and other insects, had joined the party, bringing with her a young son and a Rothschild cousin. This Baronne Rothschild was a dream of chic prettiness, entirely unshaken by a terrifying flight when the aeroplane had circled to discharge many gallons of fuel before landing.

At dinner I sat between Bobby Corbett, a school friend of Tristram's, now deceased, and Jonathan Aitken. The latter's father, who had died shortly before, I had known in early life. His mother had briefly served with me in the Port of London Authority Emergency Service, in which, I am proud to say, the standard of female looks was remarkably high. Opposite, across the narrow table, was seated the red-haired lady whose arrival had been watched with so much interest. Somewhat confused by my reminiscences, she inquired if this was the first time I had met our host. I was able to assure her that, on the contrary, I had known him for over thirty years. When my plans for the evening had been settled, Anthony suggested that there were those who would be prepared to give a hundred pounds to buy a place in such a social fandango. When I told my adventures next morning to Maurice, he agreed that anyone would have got their money's worth.

At that date undergraduates were not constrained by the rules of an earlier generation. They could go home for the weekend and, even more importantly, take their transport with them. This meant we were able to have a blissfully car-free walk round the colleges chosen by Maurice: Lincoln, Worcester, Jesus. I doubt if any other of our academic friends would have chosen such a happy way to spend a Sunday morning.

In the evening I asked Maurice if he would like me to go with him to Evensong, which his position as Warden required him to attend. After reflection he thought it would be a good idea, and we set off round the quad, Maurice a short figure clad in surplice and alb, all white from head to heels. After the service we walked back to the Warden's Lodging, and through the gloom I was appalled to see advancing a doppelgänger of Maurice, equally short and stout, white-clad from head to foot. The resemblance was too eerie to be remarked upon, even when the doppelgänger turned out to be a female of the kitchen staff crossing the quad on some errand. When Maurice retired he was given rooms for life in Wadham. I like to think that sometimes a short, stout, white-clad figure may haunt the quad.

9.

THE EMPTY SKETCHBOOK

In 1963, on behalf of the *Daily Express*, Osbert Lancaster had taken a cruise up the Nile with the object of recording the tombs of Abu Simbel. We felt an impetus to make a similar expedition while the tombs were still in their original situation. Having ousted King Farouk, the epitome of a playboy monarch, Colonel Nasser was pressing forward to build the High Dam at Assouan. Besides flooding Nubian villages, it was necessary to oust earlier monarchs who had dominated the desert for five thousand years. These tombs had been built with a cunning that ensured that, at the March equinox, the first ray of the rising sun struck the altar. To make the tombs safe from the inundation it was vital to move them, but this would mean that a remarkable astronomical calculation would be lost for ever. Even with the aid of Russian engineers, Colonel Nasser was unable to persuade the sun to alter its course.

Russian aid was no token gesture. The débâcle over Suez was barely seven years old. Nasser's United Arab Republic (Syria the only other unit) was anxious to show the effete West that it could build a dam of its own to replace Benjamin Baker's masterpiece, a relic of the British domination in Egypt. A building was put up to accommodate the Soviet work force, and a timetable in Arabic and Russian marked the countdown to the day when Colonel Nasser would pull the switch.

Unfortunately the contractor, Osman Ahmed Osma, found that Nasser was a poor shopper from an engineer's point of view. According to Osman's obituary in the *Daily Telegraph* (May 1999) he was obliged to persuade Nasser that, in order to finish on time and within budget, he must have British machinery. In 1965 Osman applied to England, declaring 'Your pile-drivers have no equal anywhere in the world.' Bringing fifty British tipper-trucks back to Egypt, Osman explained to the suspicious Russians that these were transferred from another project. The trucks were hidden beneath tarpaulins when Kruschev arrived to inspect progress.

As we set off in February 1964 under the wing of Swan, Russian inadequacies must have been becoming clear, yet the news had not percolated through to the tourist trade. Although Osbert had found the Kings of Egypt 'gazing mindlessly across the desert' far from stimulating, it was his example that inspired me to buy a new sketch book and a packet of chalks. My studio life had been cut off by World War II, but this renewal was so delightful that I spent the next twenty years seeking a stone on which to sit. Travelling, as Kipling wrote, 'Out of Egypt unto Troy—Over Himalaya' I was never in future to be found without a sketching bag spattered with paint, and carrying also wine for picnics.

It was said in my grandparents' time that if one sat outside Shepheard's Hotel in Cairo, eventually everybody one had ever known would pass by. Even in Edwardian days Egypt was popular for a winter's break. I myself possess photographs of my parents riding donkeys against a painted backdrop of pyramids and palms. Legends of clan gatherings at Assouan had been rendered intricate by the mixed ages of large families. As it happened, our fellow travellers on this Nile cruise included Grandy Jersey, son of my mother's elder brother, and his third wife, Bianca.

With the Jerseys, we watched the Southern Cross shining serenely in rebuke to some vulgar sputnik trundling across the sky. I remembered that when my father was serving in South Africa he would think of the new bride he had left behind him. When he returned, he gave her a brooch of the Southern Cross set in diamonds in memory of nights on the veldt. When he left for what was then known as the Mediterranean Expedition (subsequently famous as the disastrous Gallipoli campaign), he may have had a premonition that he would not return. As one last gift my father had a brooch made of the Expedition's emblem. Left a widow, with six children under thirteen, my mother bequeathed both brooches as heirlooms to pass down in her husband's family.

To leap across half a century, BOAC still lapped its passengers in the luxury of armchairs with wide arms, and cabin service which included champagne. Swan put the tour up at the Skyways Hotel, and gave a cocktail party the night before take-off. Here drama was provided by Sir Mortimer Wheeler, unusually gaunt after an attack of pneumonia. His account of his illness was almost surreal, his doctor having assured him that he should have been dead by any medical rules. Rik himself, sparing no details, assured his audience that on the approach of the Reaper 'one becomes a public lavatory'. Next morning, February 16th, snow was burnt off the wings of our chartered BOAC plane. For once we felt that, weather-wise, we were going in the right direction. While we waited for the snow to be cleared, an incoming flight from New York disgorged its passengers. First, stumping up the ramp, came Emma Tennant and Christopher Booker, at that time married to each other. They were followed by Harold Caccia, British Ambassador in Washington, with a secretary by his side. Harold was born on the same day of the same year as Anthony, so it was always interesting when the paths of twin Sagittarians crossed. Even Brian Wright, Swan's infinitely resourceful courier, was impressed by these encounters. 'Do you know *everyone* on that plane?' he said with visible respect.

Landing at Cairo Airport, the Egyptian night wrapped the traveller as if in the softest of blankets, a delight that the depressing cuisine of the Nile Hilton was powerless to spoil.

Even the end of Ramadan could not really be considered an excuse for Swiss roll filled with unappetising fish. On the other hand the view from the hotel's eighth floor of pyramids isolated in the flood lighting was exactly what I needed to start me on twenty years of illustrating a travel diary. My first sketch was a drawing of a tented camp, beside which was posted the warning, NO PHOTO. ARMY SPOT.

The Australian guest lecturer on the Egyptian tour, Dr Veronica Seton-Williams, had, she told us, decided to become an archaeologist rather than a debutante in Melbourne society. This was a wise decision as she was on the friendliest of terms with the local guides, veterans of many Nile cruises. She herself favoured a voluminous divided skirt, assuring the females of our group that they would have a nasty shock had they been able to understand the comments passed by the guides on ladies in trousers or shorts. Veronica Seton-Williams laid down the first law of Egyptian archaeology: never identify a site under a date palm. The economy of a village might depend on this precious tree, and the compensation would be astronomical.

My grandmother's dictum about Shepheard's Hotel could, in 1964, be applied to the Nile Hilton. Besides numerous acquaintances glimpsed in the lift, we found ourselves having lunch with Agi and Miki Sekers at whose West Cumberland Silk Mills Tristram and later John worked. Finally we greeted Jane and David Barran, tenants of Mells Manor, our nearest neighbours in Somerset.

Looking for a night club in a foreign city is apt to be a depressing experience, but the Nile Hilton had its night club on the premises, although the belly dancers had had their impact reduced by Colonel Nasser's Puritanism. They had been forced into red silk pyjamas which left a great deal to the imagination. A couple who chanced to appear in the same photograph as Anthony and me were distinctly coy about being recorded as watching the erotic writhings. ' I don't know what they'll say in the City,' the husband said. Anthony was delighted when the same fellow traveller remarked, 'I can understand when people like you and me, who have had time to make their money, can afford to come on this trip, but how do these young people manage to do it?' Anthony felt charmed at the idea of the rewards of literature being equated with the rewards of the City.

R. K. Swan saw us off to Luxor with the words 'Egyptian trains have square wheels'. Mr Swan himself had, as it were, graduated to tourism through controlling trains during World War II. There was even a legend that he had been heard, on the telephone, to instruct the traffic controller at Dijon how to set the points to allow through passage for the Swan's Hellenic Special Train. An additional warning about Egyptian trains from Miki Sekers was to take a sleeping pill. Both he and Mr Swan were right.

At Luxor gharries took us to the *SS Soudan,* untouched in style since 1910. When on board, and settled with my empty sketch book, I discovered that there is nothing like a Nile boat for sharpening up one's drawing technique. The boat's speed was swift and inexorable, no second thoughts possible and no second lines admissable.

The most exciting carving at Dendra was a supposed portrait of Cleopatra and her son Caesarion, whom 'They call my father's son,' according to Octavius Caesar's sour remark in *Antony and Cleopatra* (Act III, Scene VI). This concentrated the photographers but they were even keener at Abydos where there was a particular request for NO PHOTO, the inhabitants being mistrustful. Whereas photographers are an unruly race of savages unable to take a ban personally, an artist is seldom prohibited and sketching is usually regarded as complimentary.

Abydos had, in those days, one remarkable resident who was prepared to bridge the gap between foreign tourist and suspicious fellaheen. This was an English woman who lived with a donkey for companion and occupied herself in recording the temples. A firm believer in the Egyptian gods, she had lived in their land for the whole of her life, so it would seem sensible to worship Horus and his coevals. Equally sensible was the lady's habit of conforming to local sanitary practices. Night and morning the men marched out into the desert in one direction, and the women walked in another. It was not revealed at what age boy children were promoted to walking with the men.

I have mentioned in earlier writing that I have always been interested in hoopoes as birds, even after I learnt that in China hoopoes do not hesitate to penetrate a flimsy coffin and make their nests in the rib-cages of corpses. It was at Karnak that I had the pleasure of seeing a hoopoe simulate the action of a jet-propelled plane, the crest opening and closing to act as a brake. As she landed, her chick opened its beak to receive the worm brought by an early-bird mother.

Drawing nearer to Assouan the population grew noticeably blacker, more prosperous and more cheerful. I should mention that the routine twice-daily trudge to the Nile for water, a totally female excursion, had fairly recently been mitigated by the installation of water piped from the Nile. This thoughtful act was not entirely welcome. The walk to the river's bed was a vital part of female social life, and still insisted on at least twice a day.

When I was young, one of the fixed landmarks of Mayfair was Gunter's Tearooms in Berkeley Square, situated in a block long since demolished. A landmark within a landmark was the old Aga Khan, owner of the legendary triple-crown racehorse, Bahram. The Aga, impeccably dressed in morning clothes, habitually made a hearty tea of cream cakes. As his followers annually paid a tribute of his weight in gold or *specie*, the cream cakes must have served a double purpose. As the customers were mostly creamy young girls, the Aga would also have found himself surrounded by houris as promised by the Prophet.

The Aga Khan lies in a white marble tomb on Elephanta Island just below Benjamin Baker's dam. A single red rose is daily renewed, while a priest keeps up constant reading from the Koran. It was possible on our visit to see down below onto the terrace of the Aga's own villa, where a Nubian manservant was handing drinks to a pair of ladies. They were reclining in chaises longues of a grandeur the dusty tourist could only regard with awe-struck envy.

At Ikhmindi Dr Seton-Williams recruited a young Irish architect, Ann O'Cleary, and myself to draw some early carvings, possibly representing for the first time crowned kings in skins. Ann O'Cleary had earlier found herself at cross-purposes with an American fellow traveller. She had been talking about Louisburg (Co. Mayo) and Baltimore (Co. Cork) while he assumed she was referring to their namesakes in the U.S.A. I gather that comic misunderstandings had left both parties aggrieved.

The carvings were due to disappear under water with much of Nubia. Photography had been forbidden. The SS *Nefertiti*, to which we had transferred at Assouan, was not prepared to tarry, so under Veronica's guidance Ann O'Cleary and I raced across the sand, drew, and panted down the river bank in time to be taken off back to the *Nefertiti*. I was disconcerted to see that she floated on a flat keel of what appeared to be worm-eaten digestive biscuit. 'Dug out from the sewers in Cairo, I shouldn't wonder,' said Dr Seton-Williams.

Soon after this excursion poor Veronica Seton-Williams succumbed to what used to be called 'gyppy tummy' by which others had been smitten. The most popular remedy was of considerable antiquity, having proved its worth in the Boer War. The patentee, Dr Collis Brown, had presumably composed the brochure which had not been updated for sixty years. It opened dramatically with a phrase that passed into the language of the tour, 'Gaunter and gaunter grew the soldiers of the Queen.' I believe that Dr Collis Brown's remedy is no longer so rich in the drowsy syrups of the East as it was in 1964.

While the guest lecturer was laid out, Roger Barnes, tour manager and another veteran of many Swan Cruises, arranged for her place to be filled by the assistant manager who, armed with a guide book, was described as 'Professor' Kingsley. Barnes himself had the advantage of a distinctly English appearance which was, I believe, valuable when dealing with local guides. If these plotted in their own languages to rip off the Swan courier, they found they were making a mistake. With an English father and a Greek mother, Barnes had been brought up in Alexandria to be fluent in five languages. 'That must have been a very sophisticated upbringing,' Sir Maurice Bowra remarked on an earlier Swan cruise. 'Yes,' said Roger Barnes, 'I had done it all by the time I was nine.'

The Egyptian girls from the Nubian villages soon to be submerged were distinctly more exuberant than those below the dam. On one occasion a group gathered on the edge of the Nile chanting 'How are YOU! How are YOU!' Some among them had suspiciously light skins, on which freckles were to be seen. It was easy to speculate from their polite phraseology that they descended from the British soldiers stationed on the Upper Nile during the campaigns of the 1880-90s.

We now approached Abu Simbel where the mindless Pharoahs were looking their last across the Nile before Hochtief started on the delicate task of removal. The Pharoahs had been remarked upon in *A Thousand Miles up the Nile*, the description by the intrepid journalist and novelist Amelia B. Edwards of her journey along the Nile in 1873-4. She is said to have insisted that one of her attendants scale one of the statues to wash out his mouth with coffee, of which the original could have had no previous experience. At the Spring Equinox we were told that the rising sun would strike directly on to the altar stone far inside the tomb. In early March the sun's rays struck at an angle, but even the bobbing heads of photographers could not entirely destroy the mysteries of four thousand years.

It was on this cruise that we made friends with Duncan and Sally Ellsworth, who looked after John during his holidays from Cornell and entertained us in Salisbury, Connecticut, when we visited him there. Duncan Ellsworth, 'Biff' to his friends, was that rare bird an American Old Etonian. He had then graduated from Harvard after serving in the US ambulance corps which has been immortalised by Ernest Hemingway in Italy and by e. e. cummings in France.

As a Harvard man he cast a benign eye on some of the archaeological works that we were able to observe were sponsored by Yale. 'What are these Elis (Yale men) up to?' inquired Biff. The fellaheen, as they are carried away the 'spoil' from the site, kept in line by chanting a little song, of which the refrain could be translated as 'But we do it with grace, but we do it with grace.' This was more likely to keep the workers in line than the Yale song, one version of which was popular at Harvard gatherings, 'Oh mother, if I can, I want to be a man, but I want to be a Yale man too'. Later Biff was asked by his son Whitney how he had enjoyed his Egyptian tour. He expressed approval on the whole, but complained that he got rather tired of 'women with one eye and one tit.'

On the last day on board the *SS Nefertiti* some delay caused us to have an extra midday meal. The galley surpassed itself with what Osbert Lancaster had called 'old-fashioned preparatory school cuisine'. Beaming, the Nubian stewards bore the cook's masterpiece into the saloon, white blancmange or Shape, decorated with a trellis of golden syrup. At such a sight even the most stolid of the passengers broke into helpless fits of laughter.

Covered with Egyptian dust, we reached the airport at Assouan, only to find take-off held up by suspicion that Anthony was an opponent of Colonel Nasser's regime. His passport described him as 'journalist', without further speculation (Maurice Bowra recommended Man of

Letters as safer). Anthony, Mr Swan and I found these officials to be arguing as to the degree of unpopularity Nasser felt towards Grub Street. Finally the matter was resolved by filling in a form as to the paper for which A. Powell wrote. *The Daily Telegraph* began to be laboriously inscribed, but a busy-body insisted on correcting this to The Daily Telephone, a distinctly more picturesque title.

Safe at last in the embrace of BOAC, we found the captain to be unusually chatty, wishing us a pleasant journey with a promise of iced towels. Rather surprisingly I noted that we were still flying along the African coast, and thought that I was able to identify the famous Quattera Depression. This had been a natural hazard in the campaigns of World War II which both sides had decided could not be crossed by tracked vehicles. My cousin Randal Plunkett had made himself most unpopular with the planners when, leading a retreat from Bir Hachem, he had taken his carriers through the technically impassable Depression.

My guess was confirmed by the chatty captain who added that those sitting forward would have noticed that one of the four engines had been switched off. 'These machines fly perfectly well on three engines,' he assured us, 'but to avoid flying over the Alps we are going to fly up the Rhone Valley.' I had always thought that the Alps would make rather too sharp a landing, but I do wish that I had not remembered that the Rhone Valley was notorious throughout Europe for turbulence. As we descended belatedly to Heathrow, I noticed that the cabin crew had taken crash landing stations in the galley.

The following morning Anthony was due to have a cholera injection as a prelude to a trip to Japan. This was a tour sponsored by the British Council to celebrate the tercentenary of Shakespeare's birth. I entered in my diary that Anthony 'had returned home to a high fever'. His condition was hardly improved by a disobliging review of *The Valley of Bones* in the *Evening Standard*, by, as I tartly put it, Judas Muggeridge.

From Egypt we had sent a postcard to the Muggeridges, and there was no reason to suppose that the friendship of twenty-five years would be so brutally broken. In the canons of reviewing it is usually possible to avoid writing about a friend's book for which one does not care. Anthony considered that Malcolm, apt be wracked by jealousy, had found the earlier volumes of *A Dance to the Music of Time* threatened to built up into a formidable literary achievement. This might have led to a wish that a close friend's success should not be continually before his eyes.

My assessment of the Muggeridge predicament was of a more personal kind. A number of years earlier Malcolm had attacked the Royal Family in an article in a Canadian paper. This aroused considerable anger in the United Kingdom, though by contemporary standards the original article, and subsequent outcry, were positively mild. As I remember it, Malcolm's chief complaint was the polite way in which little Prince Charles and his sister waved their white-gloved hands to their mother's loyal subjects. With a certain impish relish Malcolm told me that he was in for a wigging from the 'Commandant', as he called Anthony. I believe that Anthony's restraint in making no comment was the seed of discontent that grew into a friendship-strangling weed.

10

IBERIA (LISBON AND MADRID)

'THERE ARE,' as a friend, George Melly, remarked recently, 'only a hundred people in the world.' The truth of this aphorism was made plain when John, studying Spanish for his 'A' levels, left for Madrid. He was, through the agency of friends, to stay with La Condesa de Galarza. This kind hostess, Russian by birth, had escaped to Helsinki at the time of the Bolshevik revolution. She remembered as a girl dancing the fox-trot at the afternoon tea-dances given by the British Minister to Finland. These had also been attended by John's grandmother, whose husband Colonel Powell had been on a military mission to the Finns. I am not sure by what means Miss Fenouil had made the giant stride from the Baltic to the Guadarramas, but she was a fine example of Russian survival in exile.

The dust of Egypt had hardly settled when as Anthony responded to the British Council invitation to Japan to celebrate the three hundredth anniversary of Shakespeare's birth, I planned an Iberian tour beginning with a visit to the Mayalls in Lisbon and continuing across the peninsular.

After discussing John's plans in Madrid I proposed to head South to 'La Cónsula', repaying the hospitality by chaperoning the young Davises on their return to school. I was jealous of Anthony flying first class, all paid, to the Far East, while I bought an economy ticket to Lisbon. In practice Anthony was still awaiting his flight in Buckingham Palace Road, while I had reached the Mayalls' ever-charming flat, with its view over the Tagus. As a useful book for his expedition I had lent Anthony a volume of Shakespeare's Histories from a set I had been given at the age of twelve. Consequently he was able to begin a speech, 'Last night I was reading *Richard III* . . .'

Immediately after my arrival, Lees Mayall, I was told, had an appointment to see his current boss, the Ambassador. He returned from the interview with a prospect of a posting in another, darker, continent. There was to be a state visit to Ethiopia (formerly Abyssinia) by the Queen and the Duke of Edinburgh. The UK Ambassador in Addis Ababa had insisted that he would need sophisticated help for this assignment, and Lees had been rightly nominated as the ideal back-up. From a professional point of view this would count as a posting in Africa, a required step in a Foreign Office career, brought about by a number of African countries emerging into independence.

The undeniable compliment was received with mixed feelings by Lees's family. The night before I had left London I had been with Anthony to see *Who's Afraid of Virginia Woolf?*, Edward Albee's portrait of a marital battlefield. The idea of a posting to Ethiopia seemed at moments likely to recreate some of this drama. In a few hours Mary's indomitable spirit took possession and she was selling the idea to the children as the most adventurous posting that the Mayall family had taken on. This adventure fortunately took place during the last years of the Emperor Haile Selassie. Soon afterwards Ethiopia relapsed into chaos and black night.

The following morning, a Sunday, we went to the early service at the English Church. About thirty years previously, Anthony and I, on holiday in Portugal, had visited the cemetery in search of Henry Fielding's grave. In a nearby public park full-blown flowers were for sale, still with plenty of life before them (I imagine that the gardeners of the London parks would be too grand to adopt such an excellent idea). We chose a bouquet of purple and white dahlias, to which the flower lady had added a splendid orange specimen. This tasteful bunch we laid on what I remember as a dark red tombstone standing in a secluded grove.

Fielding's last work, published posthumously, was a record of pain and disappointment. Most of *A Voyage to Lisbon* was occupied by waiting for a fair wind. Even when this blew and his ship set sail, his bloated appearance was mocked as he was carried aboard. All aspects of Lisbon struck Fielding as peculiarly unattractive and he was right to feel apprehension. Shortly after his arrival he was to be buried there, and in 1755 the city itself suffered a terrible earthquake, only months after his death.

In the 1950s Kingsley Amis, with whom we had exchanged friendly visits, published his novel *I Like it Here*. This book was based on a working holiday he had spent in Portugal with his wife and three small children. Amis's view of Lisbon was less jaundiced than Fielding's, to whose grave he paid respects as Anthony and I had done. What was my surprise to read that Fielding's tombstone was of 'dazzling white marble'. My surprise was so great that I wrote to challenge Amis on the subject. He replied with a photograph of what was indisputably Fielding's tombstone, and white it clearly was.

On my second visit to Lisbon I was able to solve the mystery when the Mayalls took me to early service. The tombstone had been moved from the seclusion of its leafy grove to a prominent position beside the church door. But it had also been cleaned of the layer of red colouring which I remembered, though traces of red pigment remained. Kingsley and I were both right.

On this Sunday morning we started for a picnic at the Mayall's quinta on the south side of the Tagus. Traffic jams and crowded ferries forced Lees to drive upstream to the first bridge. The countryside was burgeoning with yellow lupins and white iris, the gathering of which was a solace whenever the car boiled.

The following morning I disgraced myself by developing a mysterious plague. My face became the assorted colours of Fielding's tomb, first white, and then deep red. Frightened by these ominous colours, Mary summoned a doctor attached to the embassy. This practitioner was Goanese, a relic, one might say, of Portugal's imperial past. He prescribed medicine containing cortisone, which frightened me, cortisone being thought to have contributed to the decline of my brother-in-law Henry Lamb. I was still distinctly shaky when the time came to move on to Madrid.

I was not, however, as shaky as Rosa, the chauffeur allotted to the Mayalls from the Embassy pool. The back of his neck quivered alarmingly, but humanity prevented his dismissal. Had he been fired, he would have not only lost his salary from the UK Embassy, but also his government retainer as a low-grade spy. Rosa had announced his intention to get married. 'Isn't Rosa rather past it?' inquired Cordelia Mayall, aged sixteen, but Rosa himself had taken the precaution of explaining that he was marrying only for 'companionship'.

John met me at the Hotel Avenida on Jose Antonio in Madrid, still called the Gran Viá by many madrileños. As a hotel its standards of comfort and cleanliness were variable, but my room had a wonderful view over roof-tops towards the snow-covered Guadarramas.

A morning in the Rastro, Madrid equivalent of the Marché des Puces (Paris) and the Caledonian Market (London), walked off my malaise. I enjoyed the Rastro and subsequently urged a Somerset neighbour not to miss its attractions. He took my advice so seriously that he even joined in the trading. Running short of pesetas, he sold three shirts, still in their wrappings, with satisfactory results. This friend was of Welsh origin and appearance. He had, apparently, no difficulty in being accepted as a merchant of the Rastro.

The arcades of the Plaza Mayor were as entertaining as ever and so was the restaurant, El Pulpito, a seventeenth century eating house. I recalled that Willie King, one of the great eccentrics on the staff of the British Museum, had pinpointed his idea of a moment in history. Mr King said that he liked to think that Charles I (then Prince of Wales) and George Villiers, Duke of Buckingham, the favourite of Charles' father, James I, had had lunch there before the *auto-da-fě* held in their honour. Charles and the Duke of Buckingham were in search of an Infanta as a bride for the Prince, but their mission failed. Nor do I think that Willie King's fantasy was ever likely to have taken place. Like the Beaux-Arts at Nantes, where the only record of Les Noyades is a small Dutch woodcut, the Prado's only record of an *auto-da-fě* is hung in a dark passage. Both Charles and his friend Buckingham came to violent ends, but the latter took good care of his relations. This patronage included peerages for, among others, ancestors of my mother, Mary Villiers, which in later generations threw up more than one royal mistress. It is fair to say that my mother and her sisters redressed the balance of respectability disturbed by their ancestresses.

At the Hotel Avenida the concierge made the routine enquiry, 'Would you like to go round Madrid with a guide?' 'I have a guide,' I said with a flourish. 'My son has been here for three months.' 'Oh, he is your son,' said the concierge, 'He is very big.' What the concierge had thought, I hesitate to speculate, but his manner became distinctly warmer than it had been.

The tour which John and I did take together through Old Castile was enjoyably comprehensive but of an arctic chill. Fortunately I had heeded Condesa de Galarza's warning, and under a mackintosh I had wrapped myself up in a woollen suit, a sweater, flannel shirt and vest. Even then, the cold struck through the soles of my feel like a personal enemy. I had time to do only an outline of the towers of Avila, but I did manage to draw the image of Saint Theresa which stands in the chapel built on to the room in which she was supposedly born. In later life the Saint, always to me one of the more sympathetic holy women, washed her hands of her native city. She may have found it unsuitable for one of her spirit.

We crossed the Castilian plain, with a view of more snow flurries on the Guadarramas. Don Quixote had done his work well. Windmill towers were rare and lacked their sails. The tour now began to shake itself out socially and, to a veteran like myself, it was easy to spot an American fellow traveller who I betted was certain to make advances to John and myself. Sure enough he inquired 'How is it in London?', and was hardly baulked by my reply that I had come from Lisbon. The second leg of my bet was that the same chap would have a friend in common with myself. This again came up, with talk of a friend who I knew was putting on some show at Stratford-on-Avon. Although I was acquainted with its impresario, I lay low, scenting a Widmerpool from afar.

Fourteen years earlier, Anthony and I, on a visit to Madrid, had taken a tour to Aranjuez. On the bus there were two American girls who, we thought, might be attached to the US Embassy. There was also a tall young Englishmen, who asked for a seat that would enable him to stretch his legs. He made no contact with us, but the American girls obviously felt it was his duty to make contact with them,

VP drawing at Avila, early Spring 1964

although they got little response. At luncheon the young Englishman asked if he could sit at our table, to avoid the guide. In the course of the meal, we found that we had many friends in common and, even more enjoyably shared figures of fun. Jokes blossomed. On the last leg of the tour the discomfiture of the American girls became palpable. 'These bloody English turn up their noses at each other, and then behave as though they were dearest friends.'

 ' Luncheon, on the tour shared by John and me, was eaten at Segovia, where no one could fail to be impressed by the double-decker aqueduct, still in use and built without mortar. It was here, over a meal of sucking pig, that another, hardier American not only took off his coat but sent back his Coca Cola as insufficiently chilled.

Having been inducted into the Tate Gallery at the age of nine, I never felt strange in a picture gallery and I am grateful to John for drawing my attention to the Musio Lazaro Galdiano. Don Jose Galdiano never, as far as I could see, bought a bad picture and, even more unusual for a collector, never bought a *big* bad picture. Among the examples of the British school I was ravished by an R. P. Bonington, whose treatment of a rough grey sea made a somewhat hackneyed subject sparkle with originality.

On a visit to the Prado I first paid my respects to the Hieronymus Bosch table in which early examples of surrealism can be found, such as an ancient beldame wearing a thatched roof as a hat. I was studying another Bosch, the Garden of Delights, when a party of young ladies trooped behind me. Their leader quickly directed their attention to a decorous Velasquez on the opposite wall. This was not surprising as Bosch's 'delights' included sticking the stalk of a rose into the naked bottom of a fellow roisterer.

Before I left Madrid, I met John's hostess, La Condesa, at the Milford Hotel which was managed by the Galarzas. This hotel was mostly occupied by Americans engaged in the film business. Spain offered advantages for directors. The Spanish army, for example, still retained some units of cavalry, useful for historical pictures. Backgrounds on the other hand were sometimes less appropriate. In the production of *Richard III*, Laurence Olivier met his end at the Battle of Bosworth, fought in an olive grove, rather than among the hedges of Northamptonshire.

La Condesa de Galarza had adapted to Spanish life without losing any of her international sophistication. We met in the bar of the Milford Hotel, occupied by many couples in what might be called a semi-clinch. There had, however, been a stormier episode, when an obnoxious small boy, offspring of workers in the film industry, had jabbed at the switchboard operator with a pair of scissors. The blood drawn roused the Spanish pride of El Conde de Galarza. Taking off his belt, he gave the boy a few well-deserved swipes. He then told the parents to get out within the hour. This, it was reported, they wisely did, before the Spanish legal system could move into action. I was sad to leave Madrid, and John was sad not to be coming to La Cónsula, where he had already been lavishly entertained.

11.

IBERIA – MALAGA

On the imposing iron gates of La Cónsula a plaque bears the date 1858. That must have been the year in which the widow of a German consul built her dream palace and planted an arboretum of palms and avocado to shade the garden. The palace itself was in the Italian style, whitewashed walls without, and marble floors within. The family dined on an arcaded balcony, and a swimming pool fitted neatly into the architectural pattern.

La Cónsula, September 1964

Bill Davis and VP at La Cónsula (photo: AP)

Anthony and I had first stayed at La Cónsula in 1962 as a stopping point on our way to visit Gerry Wellington at La Torre outside Granada. A telegram had arrived for us confirming that we were expected for luncheon, along with Bill Davis who kindly drove us. With a disregard for Spanish eating habits, the telegram informed us, 'Duke lunches punctually at 1 pm.' The Spanish post-office must have found this message incomprehensible because it was repeated twice.

The Davis hospitality was generous. Bill collected books on a scale that left few walls uncovered with bookcases, but among my acquaintance he was unique in never having attempted or proposed to write a book of any kind. From a writer's point of view Bill was a perfect reader. Annie, his wife, and the mother of his children Teo and Nena, was loved by me, and indeed by all who knew her. Her sister Jeanie had been the first wife of Cyril Connolly who had also retained a great affection for Annie. It was far from usual to hear no cross words from Cyril about his friends, but speaking of Annie he was never anything but fond.

Towards Bill, Cyril's attitude was more ambiguous. In consequence Bill took a sardonic pleasure in the legend of Cyril and the bottle of Evian water. This happened in Paris when Bill, by his own account, was putting back a good deal of drink. Cyril called on Bill in the latter's hotel bedroom where a full bottle of Evian stood on the bedside table. Cyril asked if he might fill a glass, and downed it, remarking that it was really the best water in the world. Bill's comment, 'I hadn't the heart to tell him that I had just filled the Evian bottle from the tap,' would have been particularly cruel to someone of Cyril's generation, brought up to believe that Parisian taps ran pure typhoid.

Two years before our visit to La Cónsula, the Davises had supplied the background for a vast party to celebrate Ernest Hemingway's sixtieth birthday. This party was the peak of Hemingway's return to Spain, which included a terrible pursuit of bull-fights requiring night journeys that criss-crossed the peninsular. Bill drove through the nights in his squire-like devotion to Hemingway, the knight of the wine bag (skin) always kept at the ready.

Although there is no photographic evidence that Annie was enjoying herself at the birthday celebrations (even when a firework had set fire to a palm tree), she had her difficulties as a hostess. The illustrious guest had his routine, particularly his swimming exercise. At a certain hour in the afternoon Hemingway growled a challenge to the leanest of the English boys, 'Race you two lengths.' Unfortunately for the veteran of many challenges, the young man had swum for the British Army when doing his National Service. He flicked up and down the pool at a speed which left his sixty-year-old rival far behind. According to Annie, 'Ernest went straight to his bedroom and slammed the door. He did not emerge until the following morning.' He did however apologise to Annie for his uncouth behaviour. The 'Dangerous Summer' predicted by Hemingway then deteriorated into legal wrangles among the bull-fighters. The tragedy of Hemingway's own collapse followed barely two years later.

In a century the avocado trees in the garden of La Cónsula had grown to forest tree height. The pears had shrunk proportionately, and I alone seemed to enjoy eating the windfalls. Through this jungle ranged two Pyrenian hounds, one King Charles and an uncounted number of Siamese cats with their kittens. I watched the antics of the latter while waiting for my host to set out for market in Malaga. I had been warned by a previous guest that, if one wanted to escape the golden prison of La Cónsula, this was one's best opportunity. The market was most rewarding, and there was also a famous picture in the local museum of a bearded surgeon, in frock coat of the period, contemplating the heart which he had just extracted from the nude body of a beautiful lady.

More of the local life became apparent when I went with Annie to the Post Office in Torre Molinos. Annie, born in the same year (1912) as myself, had been discussing the sexual needs of growing boys. A Spaniard she knew had told her that, at a suitable age, he had been taken by a somewhat older friend to what was in practice the brothel in his local village. This had left him with such a pleasant recollection that now in later life he still, on occasion, dropped in at the pleasant bordello. I said that the English equivalent would be going to see one's old nanny, which Annie thought was much less desirable.

When we arrived at the Post Office, a smart new building, designed to cater for tourists sending postcards, I noticed that a gynaecologist had his surgery on the floor above the postal service; at which I made a ribald remark to Annie, that one never knew when one might need a specialist. She replied that Spanish husbands had so many awful diseases. I felt that there was something to be said for just calling on one's old nanny.

It was whitewashing time at La Cónsula, supplying a perfect model, a man on a ladder moving from one pose to another. Bill not only asked for one of my sketches, but at my next visit I found that he had framed it, the most gratifying of compliments.

In the meantime there was the prospect of chaperoning the Davis children back to school, so that Annie became submerged in a tangle of nametapes. This prevented her from joining the party which Bill drove over mountains to luncheon with the painter Edward Le Bas. A honeymoon couple had arrived a day or two before and, having settled in the back of the car, sent frissons of terror at Bill's style of driving. He having lost the sight of one eye and the hearing in one ear, I must admit that each crossroads was a crisis.

Edward Le Bas had settled in a house with superb views gazing southward to where the Rock of Gibraltar raised its horn, though nearby there was a bull ring and a slaughterhouse, both under construction. It was not clear how many guests had been expected, and only Annie's foresight in sending us with a pile of tortillas saved six people from lunching on twelve cigales. The Le Bas manservant had an ominous air of domination, often worn by those who have established tyranny over their employers. On the way home the honeymooners already began to look as if marriage was a journey rougher than they expected, although the drive had been scented by orange blossom throughout.

There was also the paradisiacal smell in the garden of La Cónsula when I rose at 5am to chaperone Teo and Nena Davis on their early flight to their respective schools. The nightingale's farewell was delivered with a prodigality of trills seldom to be heard in England. Beside the runway I saw the carcass of a burnt-out aircraft had been left, presumbably as a stark warning to those taking off or landing.

There had been the gloomy prospect of a four-hour wait at Madrid for our onward connection. Suddenly I heard a flight to London called. Teo's brilliance in Spanish enabled us to change our tickets, and Passport control made it clear that I need not be over-scrupulous in writing down the children's particulars. In consequence we were left with a four-hour gap in London before the Davises were expected by their next escorts. The only film which sounded remotely suitable for their ages was called *H.M.S. Defiant*, starring Alec Guinness and Dirk Bogarde.

The film turned out to belong to the school of *Mutiny on the Bounty*, with the additional goriness of strong colour. Guinness, an idealistic

Captain (Trafalgar period), takes his little son to sea as a midshipman, only to find that the boy is victimised by Bogarde, the sadistic First Lieutenant. Guinness loses an arm (the Nelson touch) but manages to defeat Bogarde. Indeed, if I remember rightly, Bogarde's body goes overboard in spectacular fashion. The film left me as shattered as Guinness's arm, but the children said they had enjoyed it.

At the end of a long day I was revived by my niece Antonia's invitation to dine, she having empty places for two at a dinner party. I had Tristram with me, so we were happy to stop gaps for Princess Margaret and Tony Snowdon, which may have surprised those of the guests who had not been alerted to a change in the cast list.

12.

GUEST LIST

WHILE I was still at La Cónsula, I had to write a letter in French to Madame Lanes, with whom Tristram had been staying at Aix-en-Provence. 'Chère Madame,' I began, 'mon fils Tristram a des si heureux souvenirs de son séjour chez vous . . . ' I staggered on to what I hoped would be a comprehensible request that John should follow his elder brother chez Madame Lanes. I then asked Bill, who had after all lived in Paris, to vet the result. Bill always seemed to me to be something of a domestic dictator. I was therefore amused, and touched, that he said that I would be better advised to consult Annie. This reversed a theory I had long held that any spouse is convinced of his/her superiority in command of the French language. Madame Lanes graciously overlooked any deficiencies in my letter and agreed to receive John.

On 4th May 1964 Anthony returned to Chantry after his Japanese adventure, followed by John on May 8th. There was hardly time for John's washing to be sorted out before he set off for Aix. On looking back I see that John was having what is now known as a 'gap' year—in his case a scant nine months, filled however with variety: Spain, France, and a visit to the Dublin Horse Show. Anthony's programme had been more varied, but he arrived in surprisingly good shape for someone who had, owing to time travel, breakfasted on smoked salmon and hock.

He reported that one did not know what to be a man was until one had travelled in the Far East. Anthony's fellow representative of the British Council had been Dame Muriel Bradbrook, a delightful academic, and Alan Pryce-Jones, an old and dear friend, for whom he had worked on the *The Times Literary Supplement*. He had also met an admiral who remembered my father's first cousin, Admiral William Pakenham, as a young naval attaché at the time of the Battle of Tushihama. In this 1905 battle the Japanese Navy knocked a hole in the Russian fleet and took the first step on the road to being a world power.

Cousin Willie had watched the battle from a deck chair on board the commanding admiral's flagship. Spattered with blood, he retired only to reappear in a clean uniform. He was also reputed to be a leading character in Claud Farrère's novel, *La Bataille*. Farrère had been a naval officer and the plot of his novel concerns a British naval officer's affair with the Japanese admiral's wife, and the admiral's success in blackmailing his wife's lover into advising on the strategy of battle. In the novel itself the admiral is killed in the battle, and his widow retires to the Japanese equivalent of a convent. A film version was made in the 1930s with Charles Boyer as the Japanese admiral, Merle Oberon as his wife, and John Loder the cavalry officer turned leading man, as the projection of Willie. The ending was far gorier, with Cousin Willie killed in the battle, and the Japanese admiral committing suicide with the aid of a brother officer. Cousin Willie denied the whole story.

Earlier in the year Osbert and Karen Lancaster had paid what was to be Karen's last visit to Chantry. Her loss was a tragedy, unexpected, and irreplaceable. The Lancasters' visit was followed by one from Riccardo Aragno, who had adapted *Afternoon Men* for the stage. This had acted as a feverish injection to Anthony who was diverted from the next volume of *Dance* to write not one, but two plays, *The Garden God* and *The Rest I'll Whistle*.

Riccardo Aragno had been consulted during the making of the enjoyable film *Divorce Italian Style*. On his advice what had been planned as a sombre attack on the Italian judicial processes had been redirected as a very black comedy. The hero, played by Marcello Mastroianni, is in love with a younger girl and has difficulty in disposing of his less young wife. He is shown running a tape recorder to get evidence of her adultery. Piquancy is added to the scene by Mastroianni's own appearance. He is wearing a hairnet, which would probably provoke less mirth in latin countries than it would from a crude British audience.

Told by the local mafia that Sicilian honour required him to revenge himself, Marcello shoots the guilty pair and serves a short term in prison. He has already taken the precaution of securing the judge's goodwill by sending him a bottle of wine when dining in the same restaurant. Remarried to the lovely girl, Marcello sets off on an idyllic honeymoon cruise. Relaxing on deck beside his new bride, he bends down to kiss her, and the last shot shows her bare foot by the bare foot of the young sailor at the wheel. When I had seen this film, I insisted that I could not remain married to anyone who had not shared the experience. After seeing the film for himself, Anthony agreed.

So much of my life has been spent at Paddington Station that I have never been surprised by whoever I happen to meet under Brunel's great arched roof. Nevertheless 11th September 1964 was a socially bumper day. First I encountered John Betjeman who, with what I can only describe as a leer, took a copy of *A Little Learning* out of his suitcase. This was the first (and only) volume of Evelyn Waugh's autobiography. Probably Betjeman was looking forward to a rewarding bout of annotation. In the meantime he pointed to a passing cleric and inquired if this could be our rector. Having directed my campaign to prevent the destruction of the rood screen in Holy Trinity Church, Chantry, Betjeman was interested to see a potential destroyer. Although that particular clergyman was not the rector of Whatley and Chantry, the local iconoclast appeared a moment later. I thought it unwise to effect an introduction.

Joining Anthony at the train, I found that Evelyn himself had appeared and accepted Anthony's invitation to come back with us for the night, pausing only to sign three of his books for a passing admirer. As it was Friday, I stopped at Macfisheries in Frome to buy salmon for Evelyn's dinner. After he had announced his kidnapping to his wife Laura, Evelyn settled down to an analysis of our visitors book.

As an indoor sport, searching a host's visitors book is one of the most enjoyable for a guest, not infrequently leading to a discovery of social double dealing. The names of *bêtes noires*, or even known enemies, are apt to reveal a strain on loyalty. Evelyn was undeniably impressed by the last entry before his own: 'Duc de Grimaldi Reguisse,' he read, or rather misread, as the guest in question was a young friend of John's whose name was Luc. Turning a few pages back, Evelyn came upon the signature 'Evelyn Nightingale', remarking dead-pan that he had once known her very well, she having been his first and runaway wife. In the morning he was distinctly tottery as he left by station taxi. Remembering the story of Evelyn's last final years, it seems likely that this was one of the last excursions of a novelist who had made a second profession as a traveller.

The general election of 1964 was celebrated by the traditional party at the Savoy given by the *Daily Telegraph*. I have referred to other, earlier parties, but this one was distinguished by wildly inaccurate forecasts by those who might be supposed to have inside knowledge. Some deductions might be drawn from the two earliest results to come in from the constituencies which prided themselves on the speed of their counting. These constituencies, East and West Billericay, always reminded me of Beachcomber's two pigs called East Ham and West Ham. Whatever their results, Henry Fairlie, a journalist of bohemian habit, declared that the Conservatives would have a majority of ten. On the other hand, Oliver Poole, former MP and later a peer, declared that Labour's majority would be getting on for two hundred. Next morning revealed that these men in the know were wildly off target. Labour indeed had a majority, but a skinny one of four.

Sailing the rough sea of the election party, I was washed up alongside Graham Greene, who gave me the news that Kruschev had been sacked, adding that 'we had not been kind enough to him'. This struck me as an unusual point of view, even for a professional controversialist such as Graham. I replied, with spirit, that in my opinion we had been much too kind.

During the party I also heard that Karen Lancaster, struck with a heart attack earlier in the year, was once again in a Reading nursing home. It was believed, however, that when her insulin level was adjusted, she might return home. A few days later Karen herself rang up to thank me for sending her some carnations, at a time of year when chrysanthemums were the usual floral tribute. She was in good spirits and hoping to go home in a couple of days, to resume her chronic warfare with her cook, who, excellent at her craft, was apt to take advantage of any neglect of Osbert's to lock up the drinks cupboard.

Two days later, Osbert rang to say that Karen had died that morning. Such was my sadness that I made a most inadequate attempt at words of comfort. Only when, eight years before, I mourned the loss of my sister Julia, had I felt more grief-stricken. Karen created her own background wherever she chanced to be living. To Anthony and me it was, as a highland chieftain described the Union of Scotland with England, 'the end of an old song'.

Karen had always laid down strict boundaries for her social life, married as she was to an incorrigible party-goer. Osbert might well have pleaded that a cartoonist needed to keep the antics of the human race perpetually under observation. He was, indeed, supported in this by Queen Elizabeth II who, at a Buckingham Palace garden party, had inquired of Osbert if he were looking for models.

There was one house where Karen was always delighted to dine. This was Fawley Bottom where John Piper and his wife Myfanwy lived a life devoted to the practice of all the arts. John's approach was polymathic, while Myfanwy made her own contributions with the libretto for Benjamin Britten's opera *The Turn of the Screw*. It was here that Karen enjoyed singing round the piano, while John Piper played popular songs of any date that came to mind. And it is in the quiet of Fawley churchyard that Karen is buried, still surrounded by her friends.

After Karen's funeral Osbert came to stay, with the consoling addition of Lucy and Alan Moorehead who had both been close friends of Karen. It was from the Lancasters' house in Addison Crescent that Alan had left for D-Day as the accredited reporter attached to General Montgomery's Headquarters. Alan, originally from Melbourne, had a brilliant career reporting in North Africa, and this assignment was undoubtedly a peak in his professional life.

Security had made high drama of Alan's departure for France. His kit was stacked in the hall. Outside a car was waiting. Alan had been given his orders in a sealed envelope, only to be opened at 3pm. As the hour approached there was somewhat wild speculation as to what his destination could be. The hour struck and Alan opened his orders. The message read, 'Report to Addison Road Station', which was immediately across the road and had been secretly converted into an operational nerve centre.

Our other dinner guests for the Moorehead visit had driven from Hardy's country. They were living in a wildly beautiful house, scene of the sheep shearing dinner in *The Return of the Native*. Alan, coming downstairs for dinner, was startled to meet someone with whom he had enjoyed a romance during World War II. At dinner he found himself sitting next to this lady's husband, who, Alan was even more startled to find, admitted to having been married three times. 'Have you really been married three times?' inquired Alan. 'Yes, and this one isn't going too well either,' was the pessimistic and only too prophetic reply.

With two non-bridge playing sons and a husband who had remained stuck in the doldrums of auction bridge, the game had never been played under The Chantry roof. It transpired that the Mooreheads and Osbert were keen to have a rubber. We four retired to my sitting-room, where I improvised a table and found cards and markers dating from an earlier age. There we sat surrounded by literary chaos, whilst next door in the library Anthony and Tristram remained reading in dignified and gentlemanly seclusion.

13.

OVER THE OCEAN

EARLY IN 1965 photographs arrived which were reassuring about John's assimilation into a life at Cornell, he having played the part of Ithamore in a production of Marlowe's *The Jew of Malta.* This is a distinctly lugubrious piece and Ithamore, a treacherous slave, is a far from pleasant character. The production was dressed in the style of 1531 (the play's date) and John looked convincing in doublet and hose, stretched out in the lap of a buxom female, a beaker of wine in his hand.

No one could have been kinder than the Mizeners who took John to spend Christmas (1964) with their daughter Bibsy Colt and her family in Providence. The Ellsworths, friends made on the Nile Cruise, gave him refuge over Thanksgiving, a festival which Edith Wharton has described as an occasion when everyone is incited to give thanks for the blessings of the past year. It was with thanks in our hearts that Anthony and I flew to Boston on an expedition that was to combine business at Little Brown with a visit to John at Cornell.

When we arrived in Boston there was of course a time-lag, in more senses than one, which made me remember how Dublin looked to me as a child passing through on the train. I mentioned this to Anthony and was conscious that the elderly taxi-driver's neck had changed colour. When we had cause to make some comment on delivering us to the Boston Hilton, his accent, West of Ireland I should have said, was of the softest. Anthony's allergy to manifestations of my Irish affiliations was too strong for me to explore the driver's background. The Boston Hilton had, not surprisingly perhaps, a different atmosphere to its sister on the Nile. Rooms changed over at 3pm and we were somewhat early in taking possession. On one of the beds a parting guest, male, was sitting in a state of palpable despair. His predicament would have made a wonderful opening for an author intent on writing the Great American novel.

When we finally gained possession of our room, I was pleased to see that we had a view over the Boston Public Gardens where stands an equestrian statue of George Washington. I remembered also that the Public Gardens were the background for a lovers' meeting in Edith Wharton's masterpiece *The Age of Innocence*. I was also familiar with Boston's geography from the novels of John P. Marquand. I once had the pleasure of meeting Marquand's second wife, and we had a fascinating conversation about an insult offered to her former and late husband by the committee of the Boston Library.

The statute of this library laid down that the President of Harvard, or perhaps a deputy, should be *ex officio* a member of the committee that judged books for their moral content. In Marquand's novel *H. M. Pulham Esq*, the eponymous hero has an affair with a girl working in his New York office. This posed no problem to the morals committee but they drew the line at the hero's wife committing adultery within the Boston city limits. The book was banned without protest from Harvard, presumably by the strong Irish-Catholic influence in the official life of Boston. Outraged, Marquand took an equally insulting reprisal. He bequeathed an important literary archive to Yale.

It is not difficult to feel that H. M. Pulham, the late George Apley and other of Marquand's Bostonian heroes would not have been outraged by the Hilton's easieats called the Hungry Pilgrim. And even more so by a cadaverous individual who, dressed in conventional pilgrim fashion, black, with buckled shoes, a square white collar and black hat complete with pig-tail, rang a hand bell at six o'clock in the evening. For drinks the Thirsty Pilgrim was distinctly preferable.

Hospitality, in houses and restaurants, was generous, but perhaps the most enjoyable lunch was down by the harbour to meet Edwin O'Connor, author of *The Last Hurrah*. The fish palace brought to mind not only Eliot's 'sawdust restaurants with oyster shells', but Rupert Brooke's poem, 'If you were like clam chowder and I was like the spoon.'

The Last Hurrah was admittedly based on the life of Mayor Curley of Boston, who, finally jailed for corruption, drew his salary as mayor, plus expenses, while serving his sentence. The book, which came out in Mayor Curley's lifetime, ends with an unsuccessful attempt by a priest to bring this erring soul to repentance. Curley was reported to have said, 'I like the bit where I die.' The real mayor's house was pointed out to visitors as distinguished by shamrocks carved out of its shutters.

At the office of Little Brown we were shown a framed note from Louisa M. Alcott, drawing $50 (US dollars) from her account with her publisher. This was a draft for her father, a rather irresponsible philanthropist. On the way in from Concord he had altered 50 to 100, doubtless feeling it was the filial duty of his best-selling daughter to support him. The legend was that he had to be kept in conversation in the office while a messenger was sent out to Concord for Miss Alcott's endorsement. The rather weary reply came back, 'Let him have it.'

It was a great pleasure to be collected by the Ellsworths and to be, ourselves, driven out to Concord, and then to be photographed admiring the rude bridge 'where the embattled farmers stood'. Nowadays, of course, they would have mustered tractors. The drive to Salisbury was not without its drama. I was happily helping a nephew of Sally Ellsworth to do his French prep when the engine of the beautiful Mercedes gave a sigh and died. Everyone kept their temper wonderfully but when we reached the Ellsworths' house total exhaustion set in and all retired to bed at 9.15pm.

Salisbury was everything that a Connecticut village should be. In addition I discovered that the village bookshop was kept by the father of the beautiful girl I had seen riding round the courtyard of Bacalhoa (near Lisbon in Portugal) while staying with Lees and Mary Mayall. The Ellsworths' house, a former inn, had been built at a road junction, so that its porch faced the village street; its garden was snugly tucked away behind the L-shaped wing. Biff remarked that democracy in New England required that front gardens should be unfenced; in England hedges and palings were more usual. 'In extreme cases,' Biff added, 'you could have a stone wall with broken glass on top of it.'

Of a glorious picnic I recorded the strange flowers and bird life. Nothing was bluer than the violets, nothing redder than the cardinal bird, and nothing more reminiscent of Rip Van Winkle than a distant view of the Catskills. The fresh New England air was so soporific that in the evening Biff slept soundly through a Japanese film shown at a neighbour's house. I also fell into a trance from which I awoke confused as to which continent I might happen to be in.

The next day was bright with anticipation of seeing John after eight long months. An academic couple had been kind enough to ask us to luncheon at Willamstown where, besides the University, there is a picture gallery, the gift of Sterling and Francine Clark. This had a good stock of French Impressionists. I took a particular fancy to a Renoir still life of onions on a plate. A small Corot of a young lady made me wonder if Corot's mistake as an artist was to fade into mistiness. These thoughts were provoked by the memory that legend has it that Corot painted eight hundred landscapes and there are two thousand attributions in the United States alone.

Bowling along towards the airport of Albany, the beautiful Mercedes gave another sigh and came to rest at the roadside. Without hesitation Sally Ellsworth left the driver's seat and flagged down a motorist who miraculously was prepared to take us to the airport. This he most kindly did, pausing only to collect his wife from the school at which she was teaching. On the way to the airport there was no detail of her pupils' characters and achievements with which we did not become acquainted. I only hope that we adequately thanked these gracious Samaritans. Wonderfully soon, we saw John and Arthur Mizener walking towards us across the tarmac of Ithaca airport.

Always keen on novels, of whatever brow, about American life, I was particularly fascinated to observe Ithaca's groves of academe. From my experience of university life at Oxford, the most obvious difference was that, except for a few indisputably settled and respected dons who had tenure, there was both a wish to be somewhere else and a fear that they would fail to be confirmed in their present appointment.

The party the Mizeners gave for the Powells, with delicious eats, was a study in types from across the campus, and might have been offered by J. P. Marquand or Mary McCarthy.

I was delighted to be warned against the insinuations of the local Lothario, although I refrained from admitting that I had thought them to be simple politeness towards a stranger. The President of Cornell was a guest, but I came to understand that his position was due more to business connections and fund-raising talents than to his distinction as a scholar.

It was on this occasion that we laid the foundations for a friendship with Alison Lurie which has lasted to this day. She had caught Anthony's eye on his earlier visit to Cornell, but she claimed to be too shy to ask for his signature in a book which she had brought with her. Among the many brilliant word-pictures in her novels, I have always relished the colleague reaction to a transfer to a better college and a higher position. 'One wants one's friends to be fortunate, but not all that fortunate.'

The five days under the Mizeners' hospitable roof passed in a whirl of academic entertainment. On the Sunday Rosemary and I strolled up to the house of J. O. Mahoney, the great artistic eccentric of Cornell. Over his front door there was a small dome which was in fact adapted from the roofing of an intensive chicken house. Inside, the house was of mixed periods and styles, mouldings made by the host, statues and chandeliers. In the garden a grassy terrace looked across one of the finger lakes of Upstate New York. Here J. O. had set up a telescope beamed on a road on the other side of the water, where he insisted that one day he might be lucky enough to see a murder taking place. The telescope on its tripod was flanked by busts of George Washington and Abraham Lincoln, each of the heroes wearing, as I remember, a mask ornamented with a pair of horns.

The Mizeners saw us off for New York City with the comforting knowledge that we should be shortly seeing both them and John in England.

It was twenty-seven years since I had been in NYC and, contrary to the usual view, I felt that I had changed more than the city had done. Ivan and Ayako Morris, with whom we were staying, had an apartment on Riverside Drive. Ivan was teaching Chinese and

Japanese at Columbia University. There was, in the words of the song, 'a view of the Hudson, just over the drive'. In the apartment three dachshunds and Ayako, a Japanese beauty, were waited on by a wild-haired maid, actually, I believe, a Haitian, but always referred to by Ivan as 'the wild woman from Borneo'.

At Cornell Anthony had talked to student groups, though he had been excused a formal lecture. On his previous visit he had warned Arthur that he did have a talk on The Novel, but like a wine-merchant mentioning an inferior vintage, he did not recommend it. In New York, publishing PR again took over. It was lucky that the heat had dropped from the nineties to the eighties. Anthony's latest literary agent, Harry Sions, and his beautiful wife Louise, gave a cocktail party for us, at which I had the pleasure of meeting Peter de Vries, one of my favourite novelists.

A great fan of Anthony's, de Vries had delightfully quoted (in *Through the Fields of Clover*), a saying from *Dance*, 'Women may show some discrimination in the men they sleep with, but they will marry anyone.' This is not well received by the mother of the writer who quotes it, and she asks that no such male chauvinist should be brought to her house. De Vries was also an elegant joker with words. For example, an earnest anti-racist starts a campaign protesting that a Mr Aaronson has been denied a licence to open a liquor store. It turns out that Mr Aaronson quite understands that this is a question of zoning laws, and not discrimination, Mr Aaronson being in fact Swedish.

After luncheon at the Algonquin, of which I had always doubted the existence, Allen Williams took us to the bus terminal for the ride out to Princeton. I was suffering with a slight malaise, and the flats of New Jersey did little to raise my spirits, but arrival at the agreeably ramshackle home of Beverley and Allen Williams effected an immediate cure. Dogwood and lilac were in flower, transforming the campus into a garden.

Allen and Beverley gave a gourmet dinner party at which the company talked loudly until 11pm, when I slipped off to bed. I was vaguely aware that the hosts were clearing up to the sound of Land of My Fathers and Cwm Rhondda played fortissimo. Anthony, unable to find the light switch, had laid his clothes on the dressing-table and slept on top of his bed wrapped in a counterpane. Among the guests not met before were Arnold Roth, the cartoonist, and his wife Carol. They came to see us on their visits to England, and Carol unfailingly sent Anthony a card on St Valentine's Day, showing a genius for arranging for it to be delivered on February 14th, always choosing a lacy model.

The trip to Princeton was an interlude in a hectic life with the Morrises. This included a dinner party where we met Muriel Spark in an all-sparkle dress, who recommended a grand car to take us to the airport, Anne Chisholm, a friend of Tristram's and later of John's, and Whitney Ellsworth, delightful son of Biff, and the power behind *The New York Review of Books*. We all talked and argued till past 1am. The next morning I did a little drawing of Ayako with her lovely black hair let down to its full length.

One of Ivan Morris's enthusiasms, besides his three wicked dachs-hunds, was the care of a tank of sea-horses. I had always loved these little rococo figures who swim upright by means of a propeller-like organ above their tails. They had first come to my notice in the aquarium at the London Zoo, just opened when I was ten years old. Consequently I shared Ivan's concern when the water in which the sea-horses swam had become murky. From 1937 I had remembered the Battery as being the nicest place in New York, and suggested we should get some sea water from the waterfront of Manhattan.

With a handful of plastic bags, we set off, only to find that the water was heavily guarded by nautical figures intent on repelling trespassers. The ferry for the Statue of Liberty was just leaving, which seemed to give hope that we might do better there. Then Ivan discovered that not only were the plastic bags full of holes, but the round-trip would take far longer than we expected. We leapt ashore, to the fury—or so Ivan declared—of the ferry's outraged sailors.

In the meantime Ved Mehta had been interviewing Anthony for *The New Yorker*. Ved, heroically overcoming the loss of his sight as a small boy, had grown up to be a remarkably talented writer. In the piece he mentioned the sea-horses in passing, and went on to discuss *Dance*, now in its seventh volume. The result was an indignant letter from an American friend not heard of for ten years. How dared we come to NYC without calling him up? It was awkward to explain that we had been credibly informed that this friend had died in sad circumstances. I wrote rather devious apologies, explaining we had heard that he no longer lived in New York. I think our poor friend smelt a rat because a rather shirty answer came back. He was astonished at the idea he could live anywhere else.

Two days later we flew back to London, Anthony with an impressive number of interviews clocked up, most of them over meals; both the interviewers and meals being of mixed quality. On the flight, I sat next to a silent man who wore a furry hat throughout. His silence was explained when he filled in his landing card with the single world Albanian (this was 1965). The only other sign of animation he gave was to ask the cabin steward for 'Champagne' in clipped tones. There his command of foreign tongues failed him. Faced with the slot labelled 'profession', he wrote 'labour' and left it at that.

Later in July Rosemary and Arthur Mizener crossed from New York by sea with John on the Queen Mary. They had taken a flat in a Regency house in Brighton, in a terrace adjacent to the one in which Anthony's mother had lived out her girlhood. That was Chichester Terrace where the Miss Wells Dymokes were pets of their neighbour Lord Abergavenny. He was rumoured to be able to ride to Brighton from Erridge Castle without setting a foot off his own land. The top half of the house rented by the Mizeners was occupied by other Americans, an artist and decorator, everything being painted scarlet and emerald green.

On our way to visit the Mizeners at Brighton we spent a night with Jennifer and Alan Ross at Claytons, the pretty house they then had. Alan had been a cricket blue, playing for Oxford, and later Sussex. It was impossible not to be impressed by a photograph of him with Denis Compton, opening the batting in a cricket match.

Afterwards Alan and Jennifer had entertained Denis Compton to meet Peggy Ashcroft, then in a play at Brighton. The great cricketer and the great actress had had a splendid evening discussing 'audience reaction'.

14.

STAGE-STRUCK AND A STABLES SAGA

ON OUR return from the U.S.A. we were almost immediately invited to the opening of Bowes & Bowes in Milsom Street, Bath. Our contact with this subsidiary of W. H. Smith was Esmond Warner who presided over Bowes & Bowes in Cambridge, and was now moving into new territory. Although a few years younger, Esmond had been at the same Eton house as my brothers Edward and Frank, and had, by dint of falling in love with my sisters and cousins, worked his way into honorary kinship. His fancy had started with a cousin considerably older and finished with one distinctly younger, taking in a number of my sisters in between. In Italy during World War II, Esmond married the wildly attractive Ileana and had become the father of two brilliant daughters, Marina and Laura.

The invitation from Bowes & Bowes had been almost forgotten when Esmond's voice crackled like gunfire on the telephone. 'I say, Violet, why isn't your old man here, drinking champagne with us?' I replied loftily, 'My old man isn't there because he is busy writing the books which he hopes you are going to sell.' This was not entirely accurate. At that moment Anthony was engaged in writing his first play, *The Garden God*.

By coincidence, some weeks before Anthony had started on writing *The Garden God*, I had happened to meet Michael MacLiammoir in the Ristorante Italiano in Curzon Street. Amid a number of places devoted to rich eating, this establishment offered quick meals at reasonable prices. I think it must have been known to show business. For example, I once saw Peter Sellers there with his *cuadrilla*, all drinking milk out of large tumblers. My acquaintance with MacLiammoir in early life

91

had not been close, but frequent enough to feel that I was justified in re-introducing myself.

When my eldest brother, Edward Longford, had rescued the Dublin Gate Theatre from financial collapse, he and his wife Christine had embarked on a honeymoon with Michael and his partner in the theatre and in life, Hilton Edwards. The subsequent bitter divorce had been precipitated by disagreements between the enthusiastic amateur and paymaster and deeply dedicated professionals. Neither situation had led to my being on familiar terms with what were known as The Boys. However, after my brother's death, his widow having resumed her friendship, both professional and personal, with The Boys, I felt no disloyalty in re-introducing myself to Michael.

Christine afterwards told me that he had enjoyed the meeting, and I had also found it fascinating to retread old boards. Having started life as a child actor under his birth name of Alfred Willmore, transformation into an Irishman had meant for Michael an immense amount of hard work. It had also necessitated a change of birthplace from Peckham to Cork City. No tincture of Irish blood can be traced in the veins of little Master Willmore, but to one of his talents this was a challenge rather than an obstacle. These talents were far from limited to acting. He designed with force and originality, and his theatrical memoirs *All for Hecuba* were remarkable for elegance and wit.

I was able to tell Michael that his one-man show *The Importance of being Oscar* had enthralled Tristram's friends, Jonathan Cecil and Vivien Heilbron. They were both fresh from LAMDA and they were enthusiastic about this demonstration of acting in the grand tradition. In return we discussed past productions from the old days at the Dublin Gate. I remembered sitting in at a rehearsal of *Liliom* when Michael had been arrested by the celestial policemen, and another production, *Grania of the Ships*, when he had marched into a Galway sunset in the embrace of a female pirate, Grania O'Malley.

This walk through a maze of memory recalled to me only too well the pains and frustrations which attend the writing and production of plays. Consequently, when Anthony started writing what was to be *The Garden God*, I thought that I had sufficient experience of the theatre and its perils to be mistrustful. I felt apprehensive that this might lead down a literary cul-de-sac. I could not in practice have been more wrong. If the exhilaration of hearing his dialogue spoken in the Arts Theatre production of *Afternoon Men* had given Anthony the impetus, the discipline of a new form of writing turned to be exactly what he needed to finish *A Dance to the Music of Time* with a flourish.

The background of *The Garden God* owed something to sites visited under the banner of R. K. Swann, but more to the spirit of Swinburne's 'noble nude and antique'. Priapus erupts in person at intervals. His neglectful subjects, mostly archaeologists, cringe before his reproofs, but find it generally difficult to mend their ways. The play was read by a literary circle which was attended by Anthony's descendants. They thoroughly enjoyed being treated as VIPs by their hosts, and the venue turned out to have fascinating literary associations.

The first time Cyril came to stay he brought his then wife Barbara Skelton with him. I met them at the station and found that Cyril was in his most house-hunting mood. As we drove up the last hill, Cyril pointed to a building that had become visible. 'That,' he said, 'is the sort of house I am looking for.' 'Those,' I said, with a touch of smugness, 'are our stables.' Cyril did not pursue the matter, settling for a new wife, Deirdre, and two children, in a house on the outskirts of Eastbourne. In the meantime a *commedia dell'arte* of characters passed through our outbuildings.

The Stables themselves, even in the semi-derelict state in which we found them, had an imposing aspect. Beneath the pediment there was a long window, rounded at the top. This was the centrepiece of three stableman's rooms on the principle of French railways where— against all too frequent mobilisation, the trucks were labelled *hommes, quarante; chevaux, en long, huit*—humans were allotted far less space than horses. Behind the stableman's quarters, two noble lofts were needed to store the horses' supply of hay which was hauled up by pulley from the lane alongside. Below there was stabling for six, with a saddle room equipped with the usual accessories. There was also a coach house wide enough to accommodate a landau.

The first family to inhabit the Stables, a young couple with three golden-haired daughters, belonged in many ways to an earlier age. Their mother, of considerable enterprise and intelligence, owed much of her outlook to her favourite book, *East Lynne.* This bestseller of 1861 had made the name of Mrs Henry Wood world famous, the story undeniably having dramatic power. As I remember, the curtain of Emlyn Williams's thriller *Night Must Fall* rose on Angela Baddeley, a down-trodden companion, reading *East Lynne* aloud to Dame May Whitty, her tyrannical employer. Dame May was later murdered by Emlyn Williams himself, a page-boy turned serial killer. Meeting Dame May Whitty in Hollywood, I was able to tell her how much the play had frightened me, and asked if she had felt such alarm. She said not when she was acting, but when she saw the film made from the play she had been truly terrified.

Nothing so violent was brought on by reading *East Lynne* at the Stables, but there were family dramas induced by the addition of a kindred in numbers which it was wiser not to count. At one moment I could not deny that fifteen humans, approximately, were relying on one cold-water tap and one chemical closet. When I was at the London School of Economics, my tutor had been apt to assert that, living in the country, I had no knowledge of what bad housing really meant. This family settlement gave me the opportunity to learn. On the other hand I have preserved a brilliant memory of a group of children gathered round a board game in one of the lofts. The youngest was wearing a crown of gold paper on top of her golden curls. Only a Victorian painter of the most extreme sentimentality could have done justice to a scene of such uninhibited enjoyment.

After a period when the painter Tim Gibbs used one of the lofts as a studio, rewarding us with some stunning paintings of Chantry Pond, renovating the Stables was an obvious necessity. This took place on a limited scale, and by some now forgotten means we learnt that Lieutenant General Sir Brian Horrocks, with his wife Nancy, were looking for a temporary home while a house they had bought in the neighbourhood was made habitable. The Horrockses moved into a dwelling which now at least had basic mod cons.

Brian Horrocks's career had reached a dazzling peak at the battle of El Alamein and the subsequent advance to Tunis. He has told the story in his own book, *A Full Life*. After being wounded, a piece of shirt had been sewn up inside him. This had impaired his health when he returned to duty, and he was plagued by the idea that his part in the assault on Arnhem had been hampered by his physical debility. As far as I know, this was a misconception on Horrocks's part. Many have been blamed for failures at Arnhem but this general has not been judged outstandingly culpable.

Brian's retirement from the army had been followed by a spell as Black Rod, the officer who maintains discipline in the House of Lords under the Lord Chancellor. In this capacity he had to escort beautiful Vivien Leigh (not, I fancy, in handcuffs) from the Chamber. She was making a demonstration about a brutal plan which would involve the demolition of St James's Theatre.

During the year which the Horrockses spent at the Stables, it would be difficult to describe their garden as anything but wild. There was, however, a ruin of a shed of which the walls were still standing. In this shelter on top of a bed of rubble and nettles, Brian and Nancy spread a plastic sheet on which to sunbathe. It was never clear how total was their exposure, but they were known to have been discomposed when our forestry adviser, retired from service in India, walked past. 'The General pulled rank on me,' this poor chap remarked despondently. In fact I do not think the General was aware how much he was exposed to public gaze, even indoors. An American friend, going for an early morning stroll, remarked that she had seen the general 'in his shorts', which of course in America signifies underpants.

Nancy Horrocks, who painted with considerable authority, though with disarming modesty, supported her husband in his wish for seclusion. Brian's explanation, that he had no desire to extend the circle of his acquaintances, was summed up in his wish not to be asked to shoot. 'I may be a general,' he said, 'but I do not enjoy killing things.' We agreed that we would not force any of our neighbours on him, though his reputation made many anxious to meet him. An exception was made for our dear friends Lees and Mary Mayall. I explained that

Lees, Vice-Marshal of the Diplomatic Corps and Head of Protocol, had such a tough official life in London that all he wanted was to relax, and that there would be no reciprocation. I overlooked that this was the year in which the Mayalls gave their Biennale, inviting all to whom they owed hospitality. The Horrockses, inevitably, met the neighbours at full strength. I do not know if it was in revenge, but when we were invited to drinks at the Stables, Brian mixed martinis that would have pierced the armour of one of Rommel's tanks.

Our next tenants were a young married couple with a small son; they kept the blinds down most of the day unlike the Horrockses. They were followed by another couple, with a daughter and a labrador, who struck a balance between over- and under-exposure as far as their private lives were concerned. Finally Tristram and Virginia, newly married, together with John, were given the Stables which down the years have been converted into an admirable house whose architecture Cyril Connolly would have envied.

15.

MOROCCAN SLIPPERS

IT MIGHT be said that we went to Morocco by accident. W. F. & R. K. Swan had planned a tour of India and Pakistan for which we had booked. Unfortunately Pakistan and Hind (India) decided to be at war, and we were left with a holiday gap to fill. Morocco was offered in place of India, and in consequence we found ourselves fog-bound at London Airport for a period which seemed likely to extend to infinity.

Few people avoid being smitten with some malady during a holiday, but I seem to have a practice of falling ill before the start. On this occasion I found that four hours in the non-world of Heathrow, followed by a 'quart de champagne' at Orly brought about miraculous cure.

When leaving our address with Tristram, he had been impressed with the romantic sound of Hotel L'Atlantique, Casablanca. The town fulfils its promise for the ocean sweeps its shores, and I was confident that the swallows weaving round the hotel were migrants from Somerset. The souk or medina could well have been the one where, in the film *Pepe le Moko* (1937), Jean Gabin played cat and mouse with the chief of police. His patrol of the souk was monitored by recumbent beggars who, as I remember, signalled the arrival of the police by knocking in sequence on the iron gratings.

The railway station at Casablanca, from where we set off for Marrakesh, was modern, clean and empty. The train, on the other hand, was obviously of the rolling stock left over from the days of the French protectorate. Attached to some of the luggage was an iron panel with grating and the legend 'Chien Pour', and a space for the dog's destination to be chalked in. We chugged cosily through the

97

flat country and on among the red rocks. The peacefulness of seeing practically no cars was soothing. I had a theory that there was a group of Roman ruins somewhere in Morocco, but we had no compulsion to go and look for it.

The most interesting sight was that of six men carrying a conical hut with only their twelve feet showing, a strange, almost balletic spectacle. At Marrakesh, the Hotel Menara was recovering from the filming of *Our Man in Marrakesh*, with Terry-Thomas (wearing co-respondent shoes and an Old Etonian tie) and Wilfred Hyde White in an unusually villainous role. Mr Sanguinetti, Bland's agent in Casablanca, had alerted *la direction* and we were given, if not star treatment, a bunch of flowers and a drink on the house. I noted that Marrakesh smelt of wet camel, but a recompense was the free show at Djemaa el-Fna. The name translates 'Réunion des Trépassés', and there the heads of these unfortunates were displayed. We happened not to be carrying cameras and so found we could watch the goings-on unpestered. The display read like a paragraph from Burton's *Anatomy of Melancholy*: dancers, storytellers, conjurers, quacks, prophets, snake charmers. These last were perhaps the most primeval, a central figure holding his squatting audience with an art that might have been Sheherazade's, painted by Delacroix. I bought a pair of slippers in the souk, haggling in what seemed to be acceptable Moroccan French, only to find that with a non-identical pattern, a pair they were certainly not.

On our way from the Djemaa el-Fna to the Hotel Mamounia, a celebrated haunt of Sir Winston Churchill, we strayed into the school quarter at exactly the hour of release. The problems of supplying lavatories had not bothered the authorities, judging by the way a herd of small boys rushed out and relieved themselves *en masse* on the sandy road. The Mamounia had a garden that was the image of the garden at La Cónsula and smelt just as sweet. Its halls were vast, having the ghosts of departed statesmen.

At the more modest Menara, I sat on a balcony waiting to sketch the High Atlas mountains. When the clouds lifted and life outside the hotel became visible, a scuffle was revealed. The combatants were impartially arrested and removed to a police wagon. It was shortly afterwards that the well-known cry of 'Hello, Tony' was heard; Anthony's old friend Lionel Perry then appeared with two female friends. When they left they staged a scuffle for our benefit.

Drifting up to Asni in the foothills of the High Atlas, we paused for me to do a drawing of a mosque and its surrounding village, said to be a favourite view of Sir Winston Churchill, honorary Royal Academician. I found that on the whole landscape painters were ignored in Morocco, but I do not suppose Sir Winston and his security guards had passed unnoticed.

After we chugged back to Casablanca we then set off on a bus trip back to Fez by way of Meknes. Anthony's limerick follows:

> There was an old person of Meknes
> Who bought a young lady a necklace
> In spite of his trust
> In the curve of her bust
> She proved vulgar, impatient and feckless.

Five hours got us to Fez where the Jamai Palace on the walls of the old city did, in those days, still retain some aroma of the *Arabian Nights*. Unexpected staircases led to alcoves with divans covered with carpets. At four in the morning the first muezzin call to prayer was answered from minaret to minaret. In Fez the calls to the faithful were taken up by the cats in their own language.

When the French left Morocco they left a tradition of many dishes on the table but not, alas, the culinary skill, resulting in the food being at best edible, at worst frankly nasty.

On the way to Fez I looked longingly at a stall with brochettes, freshly roasting, smelling almost unbearably appetising, mini footballs. Next morning a guide to the Medina introduced himself with the endearing enquiry, 'Now Sir, are you in business or government service?' Anthony's reply that he was by profession a writer, was cheerful news to our conductor. He led us to a library whose shelves, beautiful in silver grey wood, were stacked with what seemed to be bundles rather than books.

A few words with the librarian was translated into a polite hope that Anthony's books might, some day, be among the reading matter available. I found that the guide took an interest in my sketchbook and wrote captions for me in French and Arabic. When we parted he was kind enough to say that it was agreeable to escort people who did not only want him to bargain for cheap brassware.

Sitting sketching with the younger generation of Fez was less agreeable. We were taken for an evening stroll when a troop of small boys joined us. The road chosen happened to be a road on which people were returning for work to their villages, mostly on donkeys. The djellaba-clad young boys solemnly warned us against 'cents des voleurs'. As we walked back to the Jamai Palace, for some distance the road was invisible from the market above. Demonstrations of peeing were followed by the tentative throwing of a stone, accompanied by a chant, 'Fug Fug, M'sieur, Fug Fug, M'dame.'

The books we had taken with us—*The Koran, La Cousine Bette* (Anthony found this rich with recognisable characters), *The Mandelbaum Gate* by Muriel Spark, also *Selections from Browning*—this last had an influence on the development of *Dance*. Anthony was struck by the lines, 'Think first, fight afterwards, the Soldier's art'. Together with a djellaba worn as a dressing-gown, these were our souvenirs of Morocco.

APPENDIX

*

DINNER AT CARLYLE SQUARE

At Osbert Sitwell's dinner-parties the food and drink was always abundant and delicious. He once objected to me that his cook had chosen a 'nursery pudding' without consulting him. The pudding itself, a melon filled with ice-cream, did not strike me as particularly typical nursery food, nor did it seem that Osbert refused the delicious *mélange*.

The guests were an adventurous mixture, and when Edith was present, an element of strife dating from nursery days spiced up the social cocktail. I think that she was absent when Osbert appealed to Anthony and myself to dine as Molly and Desmond MacCarthy were invited together. Molly MacCarthy's deafness made her reluctant to dine out. Indeed, I afterwards learnt that when she did, she was liable to voice her resentment at Desmond's social excursions. I remember the evening as quiet but rather sad. Desmond may well have felt apprehensive as to what Molly would say next.

Some years later (during the war) I shared a house with Alison Andrews, left a widow by the death of Alan Blakeway, her first husband, a don at Corpus Christi College, Oxford. Before her remarriage to Anthony Andrews, a don at Pembroke College, Oxford, she had rented the basement of the MacCarthys' house in Wellington Square.

Cyril Connolly, a protégé of Desmond MacCarthy's, had heard that there was a tenant in the Wellington Square basement and enquired who this might be. 'A very old clergyman's widow,' said MacCarthy, and then, warming to his subject, he added, 'It will be easy for her to get in and out.'

Shortly afterwards Cyril was introduced to Alison and she told him where she lived. Alison had a resemblance to Manet's beer-serving waitress and Cyril much enjoyed his mentor's fantasy.

At a more eccentric dinner I was the only female among a party which include Daniel Macmillan, Osbert's current publisher, Tom Balston, formerly Osbert's publisher at Duckworth's, and Osbert's accountant, besides Anthony and myself. I do not remember that Daniel Macmillan did more than sink into a pleasant stupor induced by Captain Sitwell's pleasant wine. Osbert's accountant on the other hand obviously felt that he had been conned into accepting an invitation to what he assumed was an all-male occasion. His references to his wife were frequent and nervous.

Tom Balston was in belligerent mood. He had served with Anthony's father in World War I and, as a partner in Duckworth's, had been responsible for Anthony's employment there. By the time Anthony and I married he had parted with some acrimony from Gerald Duckworth and concentrated on his own art collection and his painting.

Although Tom had inherited adequate private means from his father, he had a concentrated distaste for his male parent which he seemed to expect to be a general rule. On this occasion he approached me with some ferocity, 'I am sure your father was awful, wasn't he?' As it happened my father was killed at Gallipoli when I was three years old, so I was hardly in a position to judge.

The only adverse opinion had come from a dancing partner of my mother's who had felt rejected on her marriage. I did my best to modify Tom's trenchant denunciation of fathers but Osbert thought it prudent to withdraw me to a sofa in the back part of his drawing-room.

The next dinner party at 2 Carlyle Square was attended as usual by David Horner, Osbert's longtime live-in companion, Edith Sitwell, not yet a dame, and Dorothy L. Sayers. Miss Sayers was at the height of her fame as the creator of Lord Peter Wimsey, the aristocratic detective. I presume another male was present but he has slipped through a gap in my memory.

Among Lord Peter Wimsey's gifts was an ability to identify wines concealed in napkins, together with the particulars of the year. This, Miss Sayers felt, had put her on her mettle as a wine expert. When Edith and I returned with Miss Sayers to the drawing-room she was in high spirits and eager to examine the variety of delicate objects collected by Osbert.

The novelist was of stalwart build and her broad face was badged by a pince nez. She was wearing a sleeveless dress in peach velvet which would be a tight fit for the slimmest of girls. The drawing-room floor was uncarpeted except for a few scattered rugs. Miss Sayers leapt on her knees into an armchair, the better to examine some fragile object. The chair shot across the room but by a miracle there was no crash of glass and china. Edith and I looked on like grown-ups unable to control an unruly child.

A more vivid reprise of this scene took place at a subsequent dinner party at which Edith and David Horner were again present. The other guest was Christabel Lady Aberconway, to whom Osbert was much attached, but who was regarded as somewhere between a joke and a menace by the rest of the Sitwells. Her manner was emphatic, almost staccato, becoming more so as the evening wore on and wine raised her spirits.

Osbert had conventional ideas of protocol and so, as the daughter of an earl takes precedence over the wife of a baron, I was sitting on the host's right. It became clear that introductions had been confused. Christabel, who did later become a friend, was very much dressed for the occasion. (As I was working on the shopping side of the *Evening Standard*, I could recognise from which couture house her splendid gown had come.) She found herself unexpectedly seated on her host's left and emphasised dissatisfaction by her behaviour. Leaning round Osbert's solid frontage, she inquired, 'Don't you agree, Mrs Powell?' continuously throughout the meal. Edith was loving the situation but I fear that Osbert was rather in agony as he felt that he was unjustly suspected of a social slip. Upstairs, I would have been prepared to let the situation develop as Christabel's fancy dictated, and at first it did so. Christabel told us how she had taught her younger daughter to go down to dinner on her partner's arm. 'You count the steps again, and say another word to your partner.' This was demonstrated by sailing across the room, again to the peril of the glass and china.

Edith now found it impossible to let well alone, and began to bring my family into the conversation. Christabel, catching a reference to Ireland, inquired 'And have you some wonderful Irish peasant blood?' I should have been delighted had I been able to admit it, but cannot feel that my appearance suggested such a descent. I replied that I did not think it very likely as my family had only been in Ireland for 300 years. We were then joined by the gentlemen and Osbert moved Christabel to a distant sofa.

The next day the telephone rang. A voice said, 'This is Lady Aberconway. I would like to ask Mr Powell what was Mrs Powell's name before she was married?' It was of course Edith, thoroughly enjoying herself and happily summing up Lady Aberconway in Edwardian style as 'a goose'.

Years later Anthony and I returned to 2 Carlyle Square, by then divided into apartments. One had been rented by the family of Maggie Lewis, a sweet girl who had come into our lives through a fan letter to Anthony.

I was reminded of Osbert's complaint of his pre-war stocking-up of soap, large quantities of Roger et Gallet. This he had told his staff to send to Renishaw, his Derbyshire home, ignoring the jealous feud that raged between his establishments. As the war went on, Osbert with Edith retired to Renishaw where in due course he demanded why soap cakes of Roger et Gallet were not available.

I suspect with smugness he was told that, having in the past complained of a smell of furniture polish, it had been assumed at Renishaw that the soap sent from London was for household rather than bath purposes. This might be said to be a typical Sitwellian situation, in which two warring sides both managed, without an armistice, to score off their employer by failing deliberately to communicate with each other. At least the reputed ghosts of Renishaw may have appreciated the rich scents of Bond Street.

SKETCHBOOK DIARY

Selected openings

Dendra : Gateway   Feb 2

...dos, a Ptolemaic site has a supposed portrait of Cleopatra & her son Caesarion. Fine view from the top. Two police on horses chesnut & grey were trotting around to keep the baksheesh hunters back. The trouble with this boat is the appallingly boring ideas which one feels are going on in everybody's minds.

Abydos

18
Feb 25

Tombs of the Nobles

Doctor V. Seton Willi

Abond: senior
(guide)

Frieze of Nubian and Jewish captives. Tomb of Ramose ca. 1370 BC

25th A 7.45 a.m start to the west bank and a visit
to the Tombs of the Nobles & Valley of the Queens.
The paintings in the tomb of Menna appeared to me to
be the happiest. Grandy, Major Young & I sat in
the Rest house while Tony walked to Sennufer's tomb.
out-bored all comers. After a bottle of
white Ptolemy for luncheon (the first bottle had
to be sent back as unsatisfactory) we baked
ourselves on deck. ? Saw a pied kingfisher
on the way to the Valley of the Queens

Curse on the Egyptian model for the Coiffeur at the Winter Palace Hotel?

May you cease to exist
May your business cease to exist
May your lacquer spray cease to exist
May your hair drier cease to exist
May you cease to exist
May your shampoo cease to exist

May your curlers cease
May your towels cease to
May your comb cease to
May your unguents cease
May you cease to ex

Feb 26th   Esna Barrage,   7. 30 a.m.
Snake charmer.   It is not so much
charming as bullying.

Esna, Ptolemaic Temple of Khnum.

Relief from columns in the decadent, very romanised
temple at Esna

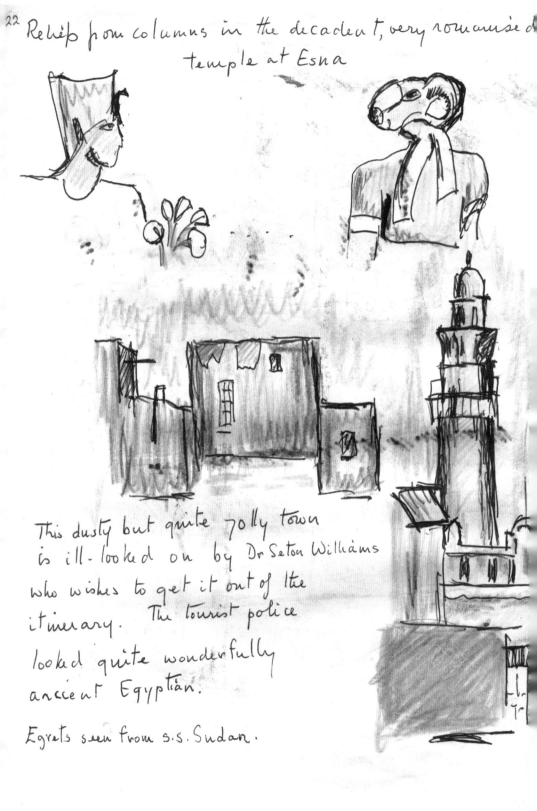

This dusty but quite jolly town
is ill-looked on by Dr Seton Williams
who wishes to get it out of the
itinerary. The tourist police
looked quite wonderfully
ancient Egyptian.

Egrets seen from s.s. Sudan.

Edfu Temple of Horus (begun 237 BC Ptolemy III)

most complete of temples " finished 212 - i 7 BC

" 176 BC

142 B.C Ptolemy IX

..day the replacement

doctor developed a nasty cold and

at huddled in a mackintosh. If he goes to the

next world shall we have to make a mummy of him.

Amenhoteph III. XXIII Dynasty

Goddess of the
Inundation,
on outer wall
of small
chapel.
The paintings
will be
removed
before
the new
inundations
but it is very
unlikely that
they will
survive the
process.

In the temple (XIX Dyn
the Copts took over and add
arches to the dromos.
Also they painted a picture
of St Peter between two
portraits of Ramses II
offering lotus flowers.

The drawings were on
plaster deeply carved and
retaining a lot of colour
exceptionally well draw

Feb 29th   At Ikhmindi Doctor Seton-Williams Ann O'Clear
and I walked round an inlet of the Nile amid
clouds of birds to find that the Egyptian Department
of Antiquities had ~~outlined~~ filled in some very early carvings
with white paint. This helped us to draw them
as there was little time, though the view
of the Byzantine Fort was well worth the walk.
The carvings were ~~of~~ difficult to identify, possible
kings in skins? We were taken off by boat
and hauled on board amid badinage.

March 1st **Amada**   Sad to say Doctor Seton Will—
took to her bed and Mr Kingsley read
aloud from Baedaker which was
like taking a service and indeed
it was Sunday. The Temple
was small, but the drawings were
lively. The custodian lives on
the other side of the river as
the previous one was eaten by wolve—

March 1st, Unscheduled stop at ~~Karanog~~ Afya to see a Neolithic village where there was a crowd of female villag came millin round,

Some passenger threw the soap presented by swa 4711 to the crow Tony cannot dec if he would be better if he di not feel enrag by such behav At the end o the visit the good ship Nefert stuck on a sand bank and had to be poled and oared off by the crew

Local officials

Local Belles

Local Schoolmaster at ~~Karanog~~ Afya, a man from the north and rather bossy.

~~Karanog~~
Afya

This man in a beautiful blue robe appeared to be a powerful local figure. [3]

On this day I discovered that
Mr Ellsworth had been educated at Eton
before Harvard and so justified my nomination
as my favourite man on board.
We also had a chat with the young Watsons
who are Tony's favourites on board. While he
was in the shower Mrs Watson told me the sex scandals
on ~~board~~.

March 2nd

Sailing north
from Adoula
this
felucca
was
sailing
south.
I hope
it was
a wedding
party.
The men
and women
sat in their
separate groups
and some one
was beating a drum.

The sadness of leaving

Nubia is more than
the usual end-of-holiday
grief, because this is the
last season when the beautiful land will be
above water. It appears that Abu Simbel is far
too friable not to collapse when it is moved
and it appears too that the German firm
of temple removers is moving more slowly
than the Russian firm of dam builders.

The site at Adoula was
in process of being dug by
a mixed bag of diggers. Skeletons
were lying out in rows, X Group
or Meroïte

the evening was spent in conversation with the Watsons before dinner and the Ellsworth afterwards. On balance to discover 2 couples of non-bores has made a vast difference to the end of the trip. Looking for the Southern Cross I suddenly saw some sort of sputnik in orbit which seemed to be going very slowly. The person who would have known about the Southern Cross was Grandy but he had seen it with earlier drives and remained silent.

March 3rd Usual scramble about bar bills complicated by the Egyptian Government's fiscal policy, but £1 borrowed from Grandy was paid back by a deft deal with the Simmons who had not previously been very rewarding. Tony is wandering round like a dog who has lost his basket. The apes in the bar are dying game and making a noise like iron filings, but kind advice for John's future given by Sally Ellsworth. (Her husband is called Biff.) Then we bundled off to see the Temple of Kalabsha moved by Hoch-Tief above the level of the inundation. Everybody behaved in a very undisciplined manner, but when we reached Asswan Airport there were R K Swam & D. F. footline to passport taken off by Hydrofoil had got bogged down in local office & when they re-appeared Tony was asked to explain for which paper he wrote, so this was written down as The Daily Telephone.

Avila [58]
Cathedral
Marble
Statue
of
St Catherine

Cathedral

EL TOS
TADO

Tomb (1518) of the Bishop
of Avila, Alfonse de Madrigal
nicknamed "el tostado" (the sun.
He is shown writing to which
he devoted his life and
which, so I understood,
drove him blind.

Mostly the beauties of
Avila are without rather
than within.

Gateway near St Vicente.

rcade, San Vicente,

From Avila we
drove through a
country strewn with
boulders towards
the Sierra Guadarrama

The mountains were
ow capped with an
ccasional snowstorm on
e summit. A rare
udmill tower had no
ils - Don Quixote must have
ne his work well

Segovia.
Acqueduct still in use.

April 23ʳᵈ '64 Madrid to Malaga

Said goodbye to John in brilliant sunshine.
He was sad at not coming too, reasonably enough.
The hotel Avenida's bill was 2156 pts. which
included John's meals and beer and wine. The
water only ran hot in the basin when the
central heating was turned off; Otherwise no compla
The flight was one hour twenty minutes
and the Davis' and La Consula are even
more beautiful in spring than in autumn

23/4/64
Christian
washing of La
Consula

April 24th

Beautiful day.
Annie, Hugh Millais's
Teo + Nena went to
see the Great Escape
in Malaga in Spanish.
I was rather bored
by all the tunnelling
but the escape
itself was well
done & exciting
Bill kindly
discovered that
my ticket was
wrong and
rectified it.
Thos. Cook apparently
were unable to cope
with Iberia's vagaries.
Postcard from Tony who had
met an admiral who remember
Willie Pakenham.

...nie marking
...hool clothes with Rosie on guard.
...pril 25th

...n the morning I did a drawing of La Consula
...oking towards the gate, which Bill and Annie
...ere kind enough to say they liked & which I
... gave to them. In the afternoon Annie
... the anklebiters and I went to the beach at

The direction arranged for the lock of my train case, to be mended which was done rapidly. Tony thinks we may be in the land which makes brass locks. The German touring party has left and now the residents are few and mostly old-fashion rather fast looking characters from the nineteen thirties.

The manager has very much taken to under his protection, so has the small tabby cat that runs the bar life downstairs.

Flowers from La direction.

84

Garden of Hotel Harmony
Oct 30th
Sketch

October 30th. A cloudy overcast morning
did not stimulate us to an early start,
but by noon the sun came out and
we walked through the (former) Park Lyautey
to the Koutoubia where I did a drawing.
Then we prospected the Djemaa el Fna (literally
a Réunion des Trespassés, where heads of those executed
are displayed) which was very jolly. We lost
ourselves on the way to the Hotel Mamounia
forgetting that all roads run triangularly
in Marrakech, parallels being unknown.
However after walking through the school
quarter (every little boy rushed out and
at once pee-ed sur le champ) we reached
the hotel where luncheon with ½ rosé + ½ vittel
was 50 Drhms, not too bad. The halls are
nasty, but the garden is a dream very
like La Consula. Sat there till 4 p.m
when we went back to the Djemaa el Fna
where we saw dancers, story tellers conjurers
quacks, prophets + snake charmers. Everybody
was enjoying themselves + we were relatively
little pestered, partly I think because we had
cameras. Walked back in a pretty sunset
find Lionel Perry (Ruth Tidwell), a cousin + a friend (Ellen Mitchell) at the
Mamounia. We sat with them after dinner and
collected some pieces of gossip.

luncheon except ourselves. The charm of
the Palais Jamai increases as one discovers more
rooms filled with divans and more terraces. (View as
The trouble with the re-painting of ancient build
in the medina is that the paint used is most
of a particularly virulent shade of blue. I do not
if this is holy or not, but I wish that whoever discov
that the shields with texts from the Koran in Santa Sophi
Istanbul could be painted a blackish green & still te chi

Nov 6th

مسجد الرصيف .

وقنطرة الخرشفيين .

① → MINARET DE LA MOSQUEE R'SSIF

② → KENTRAT LAKHRACHFIENNE

(Annotated by the guide)
I drew this from a
bridge overlooking
what the guide called
"the sewer" (Oued Fes)
The smoke came from
the workers-in-metals
fires.
        The best place
        to have drawn
                would have
                been the
                Tannery, where
                men waded
                through the
                different vats
                dressing the
                skins and
                dyeing their
                legs to the ~~thigh~~.

of the holy colour would make a tour of the
holy places of Fes.

فايو النجـري

FONTAINE NEJJAR

Brown

Blue edges

There was an old pus
of Mekr
Who bought a young gl
a neckla
In spite of his trust
In the curve of her b
She proved vulgar, im
and feckl

vember 7ᵗʰ Blue skies and balmy airs. We
spent a peaceful morning sitting on a wall in
a cemetery overlooking the entrance to the Medina
& were completely unpestered and I did this
drawing of drying the wool of black sheep.
have come to the conclusion that no meal in a
Moroccan hotel can last for four courses without
collapsing over at least one.

June 18th   Went to the Ca' d'Oro, from
the balcony of which I did this drawing
of the fish market. In the Ca' Pesaro
(Museum of Modern Art) we saw a
rather good painting of a harlequin
by Pirandello junior and an
unexpectedly pretty picture of
the Calle Rosso by Eugenio Vail
(brother of Laurence Vail). On the
way home we walked to the
Campo San Polo and drank
lemon soda near the house
where Corvo was turned out
of by his hostess for the sourness of
his description of the English Colony
in the Desire and Pursuit of the
Whole. It was a bitter winter's
night and Corvo got pneumonia.
In the afternoon in the Correr museum
we debated as to whether or not

120 Villa
Pesani
Stables
(chevaux 24)

Tapestry wall paper
in King Victor Emmanuel II's
bedroom.

Pewter shop
on Torcello June 16th

screen
villa
mi

Flowers
picked
on the Brenta
Canalbank at Sta'

or fifty it was
a comfortable voyage.
We stopped at Oriago for a tolerable
luncheon and stopped again
at Sta' to inspect the vast
villa which Napoleon gave
to Eugene Beauharnais and
where Hitler met Mussolini.

Otherwise we floated peacefully along,
the only excitement being when
five people in a motor boat came

INDEX

BY THE SAME AUTHOR

Autobiographical

Five Out of Six

Within the Family Circle

The Departure Platform

General

A Substantial Ghost

The Irish Cousins

A Compton-Burnett Compendium

Margaret Countess of Jersey

Flora Annie Steel, Novelist of India

The Constant Novelist

The Album of Anthony Powell's
A Dance to the Music of Time

The Life of a Provincial Lady:
A Study of EM Delafield and her Works

A Jane Austen Compendium